23 July 1971

For Mrs & Mrs Philip Gildred —

With regards from —

Thomas Jouvers

Diana: *the making of a terrorist*

Diana: *the making of a terrorist*

by Thomas Powers

illustrated with photographs

Houghton Mifflin Company Boston

73-148949
301.6333 0954

Second printing   c

International Standard Book Number: 0-395-12375-5
Library of Congress Catalog Card Number: 73-148949
Printed in the United States of America

For
Susan Moore Powers
and
Joshua Bryant Powers

This book began as a five-part series of articles written for United Press International by Lucinda Franks and the author. It is based partly on material gathered at that time.

Preface

DIANA OUGHTON was a young woman of uncommon character and seriousness, independent in her thinking and strong in her commitments. She was nevertheless a victim of history in which she had played no part, and which she probably knew about only vaguely.

In the spring of 1968, while Diana was running an experimental school for first and second graders in Ann Arbor, Michigan, students at Columbia turned the American student movement toward revolution. That movement, which had flickered into life during the first half of 1960, reached its highest point on May 1, 1968, the day after New York police removed nearly 1000 young activists from five buildings on Columbia's Morningside Heights campus. The uncertain leadership of the university's president, Grayson Kirk, the broad popular appeal of the issues involved in the week-long occupation, and the violence of the police together created a situation in which the students might have won sweeping reforms that inevitably would have affected every other campus in the country.

Instead, the 20 or 30 activists in the Columbia chapter of the Students for a Democratic Society (SDS) who had largely created that situation insisted that nothing had changed, that the discrediting of the administration was of no significance, that the support of formerly neutral students and faculty was meaningless if it were not total, and, most important, that the reforms which had become possible ought to be sacrificed in a gamble to create a still larger upheaval which would spread out into the world beyond the limits of the university. The passionate core of SDS at Columbia, little noticed until the crisis, had moved in their minds far beyond the reformist discontents of students who opposed the war in Vietnam, did not like the way schools were run and favored extension of the American dream to black people in the United States.

As members of a national organization which met four times a year to argue radical politics, the leaders of SDS had long since lost their enchantment with the American dream. They had become revolutionaries, quixotically at first, because even they had no illusions about their ability to bring on a revolution in the world's most developed nation. During the Columbia insurrection, however, they watched a routine demonstration on April 23 blossom into a determined building takeover and then spread to include the heart of the university, horrify officialdom and capture the imagination of students across the country. For a few brief days before the police arrived, they allowed themselves to believe that a revolutionary crisis was developing, that 1917 had finally arrived in the United States.

The purpose of SDS in the nearly two years between the events at Columbia and the death of Diana Oughton was to recapture the momentum of that week in April and to push beyond it. In a word, they determined to become revolutionaries in fact after years of revolutionary fantasy.

I had been working for United Press International in New York for about six months when I first went up to Columbia following the May 1 bust (as the police action was called). I knew nothing of radical politics and was familiar with SDS only in name, but I strongly sympathized with the Columbia students on the issues. I felt the SDS tactics were justified by the situation and was quickly convinced that the movement was broad and entirely spontaneous, despite rumors of a detailed scenario drawn up by SDS leaders at a secret meeting months before. (There had been such a scenario, but it was hardly detailed and represented less a plan than a hope.) Within the following month, however, I gradually sensed that something obscure and complex was taking place at Columbia. Understanding the issues did not really explain what was happening. The thinking of SDS, the emotions of the students and faculty who supported them and the intransigence of the administration seemed to exist independently of the issues, as if a kind of *pure* politics were hidden behind the public positions of the various parties and factions. Students felt as if they had been dead, and had suddenly begun to live; as if a world filled with hidden motives had suddenly been illuminated; as if the forces of good and evil, for perhaps the first time, were now exposed in naked confrontation. While the crisis lasted, thousands of students, officials and teachers were delirious with political excitement, some of them exuberant, some of them raging, some of them secret and cunning.

At the heart of the crisis was the collision of good and evil. The SDS, which dominated the Strike Coordinating Committee elected following the bust, clearly wanted to maintain a sense of tension between the administration and the students. With the university community in a mood to grant most of the strike demands and to reorganize itself along more democratic lines, the SDS attitude seemed a serious strategic error. The strike committee quickly split and the intense passions aroused by the police raid gradually cooled. A confusion settled over the campus as students and faculty tried to understand why nothing was happening. The moral clarity which had seemed so permanent on the morning of May 1 was dim and diffuse three weeks later.

On May 21 the SDS called another of its almost daily rallies, this time to protest disciplinary proceedings against a number of student leaders, including Mark Rudd. After an hour of tedious speeches, Rudd took the microphone and began a rambling, good-humored, thoroughly persuasive attack on the rationale of the disciplinary proceedings. The bored crowd came to life. Rudd poked witty fun at Dean of Students Alexander Platt, standing in the crowd despite the fact he was supposed to be meeting with Rudd in his office at that very moment. Platt blushed and Rudd said he thought it was pretty clear the whole business was a charade. The university had obviously made up its mind he had to go, so what was the point in lending legitimacy to the proceedings by meeting with Platt? However, Rudd added with a guileless smile, a lot of other people wanted to see Platt about a few things and maybe they would just amble on over to Hamilton Hall.

Within minutes the building was filled with hundreds of students and a second occupation was under way, although the occupiers were not yet fully aware of the fact. The parents of several students facing discipline met with Platt and then spoke to the crowd briefly. They were followed by an SDS leader who denounced Platt and the administration and said the next step was to settle down and decide democratically if they were going to stay where they were, challenging a standing administration threat to call the police in the event of another occupation. It was an adroit beginning. A debate began which was sustained by SDS leaders for five hours, despite the obvious reluctance of students to face the police and one clear vote in favor of leaving the building. In the end, however, the students stayed.

I was inside the building during most of that five-hour debate, watching a handful of SDS leaders cajole several hundred frightened students into another confrontation with police they had already seen in action. As midnight approached bus after bus of patrolmen arrived and began to set up barricades outside the campus. I moved back and forth between the occupied building, where the students were being assured there was plenty of time to make up their minds, and the lines of police outside the huge iron gates facing Amsterdam Avenue. I remember the police idly tapping their long riot sticks against the wooden barricades, each blow a sharp crack in the darkness, while the students inside remained hour after hour because the SDS would not lead them out and they were ashamed to get up and leave alone.

I had a brief conversation with Rudd and found him excited, eloquent, confused, funny, and easily angered all at once. Short and solid, with a heavy jaw and a small mouth, thick wavy blond hair combed up over the top of his head in an odd style, he bounced from foot to foot, hunched, gesturing as he spoke, glancing around at the SDS people conferring in whispering knots, running back and forth with messages, manning the microphone to make sure silence never allowed the momentum to break. It was obvious Rudd wanted the crowd to stay, but also clear he was not exactly sure what the result would be. "I've got to get back to my people," he said after a few minutes and abruptly broke off the interview. A moment later he was leading the group in singing civil rights songs and their spirits, flagging beneath a wave of particularly lifeless rhetoric, again began to rise. Outside, more buses arrived as patrolmen went off duty and were shipped up to Columbia for some overtime. It was perfectly obvious what was going to happen, and it did.

I returned the next morning and wandered around the campus, quiet again while the arrested students were in

the Criminal Court downtown being arraigned. The violence of the second bust had been even greater than that
of the first, but the reaction of most people on the campus
was far different: they had no love for the administration
or the police, but they had known what would happen and
could not understand why the SDS had insisted on a second confrontation. The events of May 21–22 had started
the majority of students and faculty at Columbia on a fitful
drift back to neutrality, leaving those most passionately
committed to SDS angrier and more alienated than ever. I
remember stopping by a walkway and looking at the gaps
where bricks had been pried loose and thrown at police
during the night. It seemed an omen.

For the next two years I covered the student movement
for UPI, reporting on events at Columbia, Harvard, Cornell, the University of California at Berkeley, the University of Wisconsin in Madison and a number of other
schools. I listened to speakers at dozens of rallies, demonstrations and meetings. I talked to students, read the underground press, learned something about the origins of
the civil rights movement and argued with friends about
the nature of the radical movement and the true sources of
its revolutionary fever.

The more I witnessed, the more I felt that what was
happening in the country as a whole had been prefigured
at Columbia when the SDS persuaded nearly 200 students
to remain inside Hamilton Hall while police were being
mobilized outside. All the issues, it seemed to me, faded
beside the fact that SDS politics centered on collision. Collision was not the only way in which SDS could have pur-

sued its ends, but collision was the way SDS had chosen. When all the arguments about issues had been made, the only certain thing was violence.

I talked to Rudd only a few times after the night of May 21, never at length, but it was clear his aim was to move SDS toward a policy of determined confrontation. The more I witnessed, the more clearly it seemed the student movement had crested when the SDS refused to broaden itself following the first police bust at Columbia. There had been other upheavals at other schools, of course, but after Columbia the student *movement* was irreparably split between reformists and genuine revolutionaries. The certitude, steely righteousness and charismatic appeal of the revolutionaries resulted in a kind of moral confusion among the reformists, who faded into inactivity. The revolutionaries failed to achieve anything beyond a form of street theater, but with each violent episode (in which they were generally the chief victims) the revolutionaries sensed their own moral superiority more keenly.

At the Weatherman war council held in Flint, Michigan, in December, 1969, shortly before the Weathermen (including Diana Oughton) went underground, Rudd called for "two, three, many John Browns." Like Brown, Rudd and the rest of the Weathermen felt their actions were morally necessary, whatever their practical outcome. In a burst of almost religious enthusiasm, the Weathermen plunged beyond politics, which measures things in the here and now, to a higher realm where the student movement could not survive. In effect, the movement died because the revolutionaries killed it. The final phase of the move-

ment's agony was a passionate aberration which cost the
lives of an unlucky handful of the most committed revolutionaries, one of whom was Diana Oughton.

The story of Diana, of course, came much later. At the
suggestion of a friend of Diana's family, and with the
strong support of UPI's editor, H. Roger Tatarian, Lucinda
Franks (on leave from UPI's London bureau) and I spent
five weeks in the late summer of 1970 piecing together
Diana's brief life. Once we began working on the story it
quickly became apparent that Diana's story was also the
story of the Weathermen, and we attempted to tell both
in the five-part series of articles which eventually appeared
in more than 300 newspapers. Separately or together, Lucinda and I went to Boston; Washington; Philadelphia;
Chicago; Detroit; Ann Arbor, Michigan; Roslyn, Long Island; and Dwight, Illinois. We found that Diana's family
and old friends were willing to help, while people who had
known her in SDS, with a few exceptions, most emphati-
cally had nothing to say.

By putting together the public record, the memories of
those who knew her, and the statements of a handful of
activists, including a few present and former Weathermen,
Lucinda and I managed to find out why Diana was in the
house on New York's West Eleventh Street when it blew
up on the morning of March 6, 1970. Diana's death, we
learned, had been determined as much by what she was as
by what she believed. Gaps in her history remained, of
course, but it was possible to watch a process of political

commitment and alienation unfold in some detail in a single life. Politics cannot be divorced from human emotion and in Diana one could see something of the restless interplay between character and conviction.

Later Lucinda returned to London, where she has continued to work on special projects for UPI, while I pursued the story of Diana further in order to expand our original articles into this book. I went back to see several people we had already talked to, and contacted a number of others we had failed to reach earlier. The conclusions which follow are mine, but the book would not have been possible without the brilliant reporting and insight of Lucinda, who felt Diana's dilemma as if it had been her own. She has my thanks, respect and affection.

I would also like to extend special thanks to Diana's family, and in particular to her sister Carol, for the openness with which they talked about a painful subject. In working on this book it was quickly clear to me why they had loved Diana, and why she had loved them.

Others who were generous with their time and memories were Joan Adams, Anne Hogshead Aleman, Bob Bernard, Barry Bluestone, Susan Christian, Patrick Cleary, Lew Cole, Doris Cummings, Peter Denton, Bill Dreyer, Professor John Hagen, Bob Howard, Alan and Lidie Howes, Lyn Kelley, Martin Kenner, Mike Kimmell, Tobie Kranitz, Ruth Moreheart, Jim Neubacher, Steve Nissen, Daniel Okrent, Karin and Merrill Rosenberg, Julie Schieffelin, Professor Christoph Schweitzer, Mr. and Mrs. Len H. Small, Linda Solomon, the staff of the Tamiment Library at New York University and several others who preferred not to be named. Errors of fact and interpretation are, of course, all my own.

Thomas Powers

New York City
January 1971

Contents

Diana: *the making of a terrorist*

The House on
West Eleventh Street

SHORTLY BEFORE NOON on Friday, March 6, 1970, an explosion tore through the front wall of a century-old red-brick townhouse on a quiet, tree-lined street in New York City. Within moments smoke began to pour from the building; a deep red glow in the dark interior was followed by flames. Visible against the red glow as people began to arrive were two young women — one of them completely naked, the other wearing only a pair of blue jeans — who had been momentarily trapped by falling debris.

Two men helped the women out of the building as chunks of brick and plaster crashed down around them. A woman who lived down the street gave her coat to one of the two and then led both of them, choking and covered with soot and dust, back to her own house. The two appeared unhurt, so the woman told them to use the shower, left some old clothes outside the bathroom door, and went back to the burning house to see if anyone else needed help. When she returned a few minutes later the two young women had already dressed and gone.

Fire trucks turned into Eleventh Street shortly after noon as two more explosions further weakened the townhouse at 18 West Eleventh Street. Attempts to search the building ended when the façade collapsed in a cloud of smoke, dust and fire. It was not until the flames were finally out, and a crane and other equipment had arrived later in the day, that efforts to search the building could be resumed. In the early evening, working in the glare of floodlights, firemen discovered the body of a short, solid, red-haired young man wearing blue jeans and a denim workshirt. He had been crushed to death.

As newspaper reporters and television crews arrived at the site they asked officials about the nature of the explosion which had destroyed the townhouse, had shattered windows as high as the sixth floor across the street, and had blown a gaping hole through a side wall into the living room of the building next door. The police and fire officials, not yet certain whether the fire or the explosion had come first, suggested the blasts could have been caused by escaping gas. While bomb-squad detectives searched through tons of rubble during the following days, speculation naturally began to center on the possibility of dynamite. The violence of the explosion, the missing women, the dead man, rumors that other bodies were still in the building and that three men had escaped over a backyard fence — all pointed to something more dramatic than escaping gas.

On Saturday, March 7, the day after the explosion, one of the two missing girls was identified as Cathlyn Platt Wilkerson, the daughter of a well-to-do advertising man, vacationing in the Caribbean at the time of the explosion, who owned the building. On Sunday, March 8, the dead man was identified as Ted Gold, a leader of the Students for a Democratic Society (SDS) chapter at Columbia University during the violent struggle there in the spring of 1968. Cathy Wilkerson had also been an SDS member and, it was reported, a member of the violent SDS faction called the Weathermen.

On Monday, March 9, detectives searching through the remains of the house found a pile of water-soaked SDS leaflets and then, on Tuesday, March 10, the badly mutilated body of a young woman was discovered near a workbench in the building's basement. That afternoon, while routinely searching through a huge pile of debris picked up by a power shovel, detectives found four lead pipes, each 12 inches in diameter, packed with dynamite.

The street was cleared, the bomb-removal truck was summoned and the search, with considerably greater caution, was continued. Before the day was over detectives found four cartons containing 57 sticks of dynamite, 30 blasting caps and some cheap alarm clocks with holes drilled in their faces for the attaching of wires. Assistant Chief Inspector Albert Seedman, in charge of the investigation, gave the first, and the simplest, explanation of what had happened: "The people in the house were obviously putting together the component parts of a bomb and they did something wrong."

That same Tuesday police found a credit card, library card and birth certificate belonging to Kathy Boudin, the daughter of Leonard B. Boudin, a lawyer well-known for his defense of political dissidents, including Dr. Benjamin Spock in 1968. It was suggested that Kathy might have been the second woman who disappeared the day of the explosion.

Early in the morning of Thursday, March 12, bombs exploded almost simultaneously in three corporate offices in New York City. A letter postmarked an hour before the explosions made it clear the explosion on West Eleventh Street was not going to be an isolated incident. In the days that followed thousands of false bomb scares were called in to the police. Dozens of major office buildings were emptied and searched. It was clear the bombers may have been few in number, but that thousands shared their hate for American society.

On Saturday, March 14, a third body, that of a young man, was found in the northeast corner of the basement near the spot where the woman's body had been discovered. On Monday, March 16, Cathy Wilkerson and Kathy Boudin failed to appear in court in Chicago, where they were facing charges stemming from a fight between police and the Weathermen on October 9, 1969.

On Sunday, March 15, detectives found a piece of flesh which turned out to be the tip of the little finger of someone's right hand. Police experts took a print from the finger tip, checked it unsuccessfully with their own files, and then sent it on to the FBI in Washington. On Tuesday, March 17, the FBI identified the print as that of Diana

Oughton, the oldest daughter of a long-established family in the small town of Dwight, Illinois, and, like Gold, Boudin and Wilkerson, long active in SDS. She, too, had been arrested in Chicago on the previous October 9; the prints taken by Chicago police on that occasion were the ones used to identify her.

When the New York police announced the identification of Diana's body on Tuesday evening they gave her address as 915 East Fourth Avenue in Flint, Michigan (the address she had given Chicago police), which turned out to be an SDS headquarters, abandoned the previous November. Newsmen quickly established the broad outlines of Diana's life: student at the Madeira School in Greenway, Virginia, and Bryn Mawr College, outside Philadelphia; two years in Guatemala, where the poverty had turned her toward radical politics; two years of teaching in an experimental school in Ann Arbor, Michigan; and finally a deepening involvement with SDS and the Weathermen. Her life seemed a symbol of the decade just ended, a progress from a privileged childhood to disenchantment with her country. American parents had long sensed their children turning against them; Diana's death seemed to mark the imminence of a final break.

Profound confusion attended the first attempts to explain who the Weathermen were and what had brought them to 18 West Eleventh Street. Their friends in the radical movement, themselves unsure what had happened, refused to say anything to the traditional press, and the stories which appeared in the underground press either relied heavily on what was publicly known or confined themselves to cloudy generalities implying that political idealism, not the confusing currents of radical politics in the 1960s, had led to the explosion on West Eleventh Street.

As newspapers published brief biographies of the four people connected with the explosion, it gradually became clear that the Weathermen were a faction of SDS who had captured control of the organization in 1969; that they favored violence; that they had sponsored a series of violent demonstrations in Chicago in October, 1969. Little had been heard from the group since; there were rumors it had either disbanded, or gone underground.

The confusion about what the Weathermen were was matched by a confusion concerning their political significance. The radical movement, expressing a natural loyalty to dead friends, generally insisted the politics of the Weathermen had been a desperate result of frustrated idealism — the fault, in short, of a society which ignored every plea for change or justice. Others blamed the explosion on a certain willfulness common to the very young and the very rich. This interpretation was best expressed by Nicholas von Hoffman, a columnist for the Washington *Post* who had been in Mississippi during the summer of 1964, in San Francisco during the summer of 1967, and at Columbia University during the spring of 1968. Von Hoffman probably understood the anger and the discontent of the young better than any other reporter for the traditional press in the United States.

In a column published March 20, three days after Diana had been identified, Von Hoffman described her privileged background and pointed out that it was shared by other Weathermen. He suggested that privilege and money had, in themselves, been partly responsible for the Weathermen's resort to terrorism.

> A rich man can afford moral sensibility; he's got the re-
> sources to buy a social conscience. Guilt, fear, many
> things can turn a rich person into a reformer or a propo-
> nent of social change. But what turns him into a bomb
> thrower, a political terrorist? In the case of our rich rev-
> olutionaries, it may also be their money and their upper
> class origins. They are young people who grew up accus-
> tomed to being obeyed, to having their own way. This
> is not your permissive psychology stuff; this is the expecta-
> tion of people doing what you tell them to do because all
> your life you've had the money to command.

Von Hoffman was not being unsympathetic, exactly, but his column was clearly intended to diminish the signifi-cance of what had happened.

The sharpening conflict between the generations during the final years of the 1960s had frightened almost every-body; people sensed a dangerous potential for violence within America, an anger that might finally destroy the already-strained sense of trust and common commitment that holds a country together. Weatherman's open cele-bration of that potential, its exultation in random violence, its refusal to believe that anything, even outright fascism, could be worse than America as it already was, seemed just the sort of thing that might tip the United States over the brink of an abyss on which it had been balancing for a decade. The explosion on West Eleventh Street seemed an omen of provocations that no open society could survive. The United States began to be compared with France during the struggle over Algeria, and with the Weimar Republic during the last bitter days before Hitler came to power.

When radicals insisted the explosion was idealism gone sour, and when Von Hoffman suggested that it was best explained by the psychology of the rich, both were trying to hold back the tide. Their explanations were intended to prove that the explosion was the result of something simple and knowable. Their explanations were incomplete, however. The young and the rich had always been willful; idealism had always contained a seed of bitterness. The explosion on West Eleventh Street indicated the breakdown of something more than the emotional balance of a few individuals.

The pictures which appeared in the newspapers day after day seemed to contradict what was known to have happened: Ted Gold and Kathy Boudin, earnest and serious, at a news conference in August, 1969; pretty Cathy Wilkerson boarding a plane in 1967; Diana Oughton reading to a child. They had all once thought of themselves as part of a movement to reform America. When they embraced terrorism it was clear that movement, once the source of so much hope, had entered a dark and final phase.

Once Diana would have seemed to be among the best of her generation. Even more than the others, her life reflected a sense of having been blessed and a commitment to extend those blessings to others. But the bomb that killed her, wrapped in nail-studded tape, was a fact which could not be ignored. Something hard and even cruel had emerged from her idealism. A privileged child of the heart of the country, Diana had died with only one apparent purpose: to be among that country's executioners. Willfulness and frustrated idealism alone could not explain her final, chilling ambition.

The Girl from Dwight

DIANA OUGHTON's first vision of America was formed during her childhood in Dwight, Illinois, a small town surrounded by the vast, flat farmland south of Chicago. Since the 1850s, Dwight has been dominated by three families, of which the Oughtons have always been one. It would be impossible to say which of the three is the *first* family of Dwight, but in January, 1942, when Diana was born, her family was probably the one most deeply rooted in the life, and the imagination, of the town. Previous generations of Oughtons had paved the streets of Dwight, built its waterworks, and donated land for the school and for the cemetery where Diana's grandparents were buried a mile and a half west of town.

One of Diana's great-grandfathers (on her father's side) founded Dwight's Keeley Institute, the first hospital successfully (and profitably) to treat alcoholism as a disease.

Several generations of Americans joked about people, especially the celebrated, the rich and the well-born, who had "gone to Dwight" or were taking "the Keeley cure." (In Dwight, it is said that Dr. Keeley discovered his cure by experimenting on the hobos who used to crisscross the country in the late nineteenth century.) Another of Diana's great-grandfathers, William Boyce, founded the Boy Scouts of America.

In Dwight, the Oughton family holds that special position reserved for those who have been both blessed and cursed beyond the usual degree. Their pre-eminence in the town did not depend solely on past achievements and dignities. There had been only one murder in the history of Dwight: in the summer of 1935, shortly after Diana's father, James Oughton, came home from Dartmouth College, someone broke into the office of Diana's grandfather, demanded the strongbox, and then, for unknown reasons, shot the old man to death. The murderer was never caught.

Diana's father was vice president of the family bank and the owner of several thousand acres of farmland, as well as other properties. While she was still a girl he opened a successful restaurant in the late-Victorian mansion built by his grandfather in the 1890s, and in 1964 he was elected to the Illinois legislature on a blue-ribbon slate of Republican candidates. A strong-willed, intelligent man now nearly blind from a hereditary condition, Mr. Oughton has always been considered a leading citizen of Dwight, for his own qualities as well as those of his family, even by those few who felt the Oughton family might have done still more for the town, considering how much money they had. As long as Diana remained in Dwight, she was, before anything else, the daughter of James Oughton.

The Oughtons live in a large Tudor-style house on South Street, next door to The Lodge, where Mr. Oughton has an office upstairs from the restaurant. Behind the house there is a deer park and a pond, as well as a swimming pool. A hundred-foot-high windmill in high Victorian style dominates the estate. The trees on the Oughton property were transplanted from an international exposition held in St. Louis before the turn of the century; an elm in front of the house was planted in 1860 by the Prince of Wales, later King Edward VII, who came to Illinois to shoot birds. Nearly a century later, the bird-shooting was still good and the Oughton children (Diana eventually had three sisters) grew up around hunting dogs who were *not* to be treated as pets. Diana was taught how to handle a shotgun as a child and often went out with her father during pheasant season, sometimes to the family's shooting preserve, sometimes in the surrounding countryside.

Diana learned to ride, she belonged to the Four-H Club, she did well in school and never caused trouble at home. She joined the Congregational Church in Dwight. She helped around the house, never quite got around to making out birthday or Christmas lists, always had some of her allowance left at the end of the week, and adored her father. She was generous, loving and strong. She was a perfect child, considered by many "the prize of all the girls," and was constantly held up to her sisters as an example. Astonishingly, her sisters seemed to share in the general admiration of Diana. Years later she told her sister Carol she wished she had resisted more as a child. Carol seemed the one always being scolded or punished, but, looking back on it, Diana felt Carol had been the lucky one: she had learned how to defend her independence.

Diana never accustomed herself to the special position enjoyed by the Oughtons in Dwight. In school the other children sometimes teased her by calling her "Miss Moneybags." When she was six she asked her nanny, Ruth Moreheart, "Ruthie, why do we have to be rich?" On another occasion, when money problems forced a girl friend to move away, Diana went to her father in tears and asked, "Why can't we be ordinary like them?" When she was a little older, Diana quietly wondered if her uniformly good marks in school had anything to do with the fact that several of her teachers rented houses from her father.

The Oughton money was a condition of life, like the heat in the summer or the flatness of her father's corn and soybean fields. The money was not enough to cause ripples outside Dwight, but it was always there: Diana's friends did not all have swimming pools, or go on trips, or make plans to go away to school in the East, or get so many presents at Christmas, or have a room of their own.

Diana's father dominated the Oughton family; he made the final decisions in everything that affected the upbringing of his children. Diana's mother was a loving presence who remained, somehow, always on the edge of things.

She rarely took part in the lively (but not exactly heated) discussions which Mr. Oughton encouraged at the dinner table. Until he began to lose his sight in the early 1960s, he was always well informed about the issues of the day and he liked to argue politics with his daughters. The children were encouraged to read, and to do well in school, and to be a credit to the family.

Diana went away to camp during the summers for three years, Mr. Oughton often took his daughters on trips, and Mrs. Oughton had family in New York and Canada; but Dwight remained the family's world. It was a world largely without conflict, as uneventful as the weekly Dwight *Star and Herald,* which reported on the doings of local society and little else. Everybody in Dwight was white; almost everybody had enough money to get along. Until the depression there had never been more than eight or ten Democratic votes in any election; since then it had remained pretty solidly Republican. The town itself is run by a nonpartisan political arrangement. Hard times have hit Dwight periodically in the last twenty years, with the failure of small farmers and the closing of a Veterans' Administration hospital, but the town has always managed to pull itself together and find something else.

People tend to leave Dwight, however, if they want to get on in the world: when the class of 1944 from Dwight's high school held its twenty-fifth reunion in 1969, only a third of the class was still living in town. Dwight is a good town to grow up in, but it is an isolated backwater in American life. There is only one newsstand in town (which doubles as the bus station), and the Gulf-Mobile and Ohio

Railroad, which runs through the center of town, is trying to end its remaining passenger service. There is one
train each way between Dwight and Chicago daily, and
the train from Dwight leaves at 3:55 in the morning, generally empty. In Dwight, the United States presents a
smiling, but placid, face. The only struggles seem to be
with the outside world, with the Democratic machine
which controls Chicago, or with Big Government in Washington.

Diana's father brought up his daughters to value what
they came from without being snobs. They were routinely
chaperoned and often prevented from doing things other
children did. They felt at home in Dwight, however. Diana's sisters — Carol, Pam and Debby — are unlikely to
live there (Pam has married a man she met in the East;
the others will probably do the same), but they remember
the Dwight of their childhood with real warmth. The
darker side of small-town life — the conformity, the gos-
siping, the limited opportunities, the sense of isolation —
were never apparent to Diana as a child. Her Dwight
was the heat in the summer, the foot-stamping cold in the
winter, the people who all said hello when they met in the
street, her friends at school, Christmas in a large house
with a large family where the tree always reached the
ceiling.

It was always understood in the Oughton family that the
girls would go away to boarding school when they were
old enough, and in 1955 Mr. Oughton took Diana and
Carol East to pick one out. For one reason or another
they decided against Ethel Walker, Garrison Forest,

Farmington and several other schools. Finally they chose Madeira in Greenway, Virginia, founded in 1906 by Miss Lucy Madeira, a stern, sharp-tongued woman whose strong personality gave her school a distinct air of intelligence, good breeding and high-mindedness. Miss Madeira had always believed the ninth grade was a very important year to spend at home with family and friends. She encouraged her girls to wait until the tenth grade, which Diana did.

From the beginning Diana was one of the golden girls for whom Miss Allegra Maynard, the *de facto* headmistress during Miss Madeira's decline, had a liking. Diana was a large, blooming, blond girl with a natural charm and liveliness of spirit, always a better-than-average student even if a little inclined to put off studying. She made friends with girls whose names were known at home, like her own, and with girls whose names had almost entered the language, like Lucy Rockefeller, the daughter of Lawrance.

Madeira was divided between a majority that lived at the school and came from rich, Republican, well-bred, thoroughly patrician old families with old money, mostly from the East Coast; and a minority of day-school students who were the daughters of mostly Democratic Washington lawyers, civil servants and foreign service people. The differences between the two groups were more apparent than real and the school was a basically homogeneous slice from the American upper classes. There were almost no Jews at the school, and no Negroes until the mid-1960s, more than five years after Diana graduated.

Nearly everyone came from a family who could afford the (then) $2700 tuition and the $1000 in additional expenses which seemed to be involved every year.

During the three years Diana spent at the school between the fall of 1956 (when she was fourteen) and the spring of 1959, Miss Madeira, an almost legendary presence, was increasingly inactive. Advanced in age, she was conceded to be somewhat "unpredictable." Nevertheless, she gave frequent inspirational speeches centering on her two favorite maxims: "Function in disaster" and "Finish in style." Every year she gave a speech on Washington's Birthday, describing "General Washington" as the greatest American of them all. Another important day at Madeira was May 19, Miss Madeira's birthday, when the girls were treated to strawberries for breakfast. Despite a trace of vanity and pride, there was no nonsense about Miss Madeira, who had worked her way through Vassar on a scholarship and had founded her school on determination and aristocratic ideals and little else. Her teachers began at less than $2000 a year until after World War II, and despite her New Deal sympathies she maintained a warm, and hard-headed, relationship with the Republican aristocrats who provided most of her students, and income.

Madeira was thoroughly conservative in dress, demeanor, and educational theory. The girls' winter uniform consisted of a white blouse, a gray flannel skirt and matching sweater, and knee socks. The summer uniform was green cotton bloomers, a wrap-around skirt, white blouse, white socks and oxfords. Miss Madeira did not believe in zippers, so everything was fastened with buttons. To pay a visit to the ladies' room a Madeira girl had to undo fourteen buttons. On weekends the girls were theoretically free to dress as they pleased, but in fact a uniform every bit as rigid as those prescribed by school policy obtained. They wore plaid skirts, loafers, McMullen blouses, circle pins, scarab bracelets and wool pullovers, *not* Shetlands.

In 1929 the school had moved from Washington to Greenway on the other side of the Potomac River (visible from an isolated point of land where the girls sometimes went to have picnics). Despite the date of their construction the buildings were all in a brick Georgian style in keeping with the nostalgia for the eighteenth century that permeated the upper classes who supported the school. The grounds were well tended, the trees large and old, the curriculum traditional, the ambitions of the school lofty but unsentimental.

There was nothing weak, self-indulgent or second-rate about Madeira. Miss Madeira's unsparing character was revealed in the remark with which, according to school legend, she had once dismissed Miss Maynard's concern that one of the girls might hurt herself climbing through the trap door leading to the bell tower from a corridor in one of the dormitories: "The Lord has His own way of getting rid of the unfit," Miss Madeira was alleged to have snapped, "only sometimes He doesn't do it soon enough to suit me."

Inevitably Diana changed at Madeira. She abandoned her already halfhearted interest in religion, irritated by the theological rotundity of the elite Episcopalianism which dominated Madeira's "non-denominational" religious services held every Sunday. She added an irreverence about social fatuities to her already-keen sense of humor, but basically she did all the things Madeira girls did — stayed up after lights were supposed to be out, smoked cigarettes, went out on weekends, ate too many sweets, put off homework, studied at the last minute for exams and applied in her senior year to all the Seven Sisters. Unlike a lot of Madeira girls, Diana was accepted by all seven, an occasion for squealing congratulations by her friends.

Diana was always more friendly to the younger girls than the average, inclined to baby fat, cheerful and light-hearted. Like the rest of her class she felt *Newsweek* magazine's 1959 cover story on girls' schools (with a photo of Madeira on the cover) did Madeira an injustice by classing it with Farmington (which they felt was snobbier) and Foxcroft (which they felt was horsier). Madeira, the Madeira girls felt, was more scholarly and serious than the others. These, however, were distinctions without a difference. Madeira, Foxcroft and Farmington were all bastions of privilege, elite institutions serving a tiny minority in American life which never doubted its superiority or its right to rule. Madeira girls were trained to be the wives of the men who run the country. They were expected to learn how to hold up their end of serious conversations and to represent the best traditions of their class and to raise children who would do the same, but no one really expected them to *do* anything in life.

Diana was sent to Madeira to be exposed to the best

people and the best schooling, and she was. The vast majority of her Madeira friends were destined to marry well, live in homes with Early American furniture, own stocks and bonds, go away for the summer, and send their girls to schools just like Madeira. During her years there, Diana showed nothing which indicated she would not do precisely the same.

In the fall of 1959, seventeen years old, Diana entered Bryn Mawr as a freshman, an open, generous girl with a talent for making friends and few pretensions. Bryn Mawr, like Madeira, prided itself (justifiably) on its serious academic tone, but, also like Madeira, basically reflected the upper-class background of its privileged students. Bryn Mawr was both proud of and discreet about its better-known graduates. The administration always refused to give out the class of Katherine Hepburn, for example, because Miss Hepburn did not want people prying into her age.

Bryn Mawr is in a prosperous suburb outside of Philadelphia, where old notions of a woman's place in the world still prevail: one has one's name in the paper when one is born, one marries, or one dies, and not in between. The serving of afternoon tea for friends and professors is an institution at Bryn Mawr and girls were advised to bring a tea service, which Diana did. Her friends at Bryn Mawr considered her terribly miscast there, far too high-spirited and easygoing for the self-important *seriousness* of most of the students. With the exception of the tea hour every afternoon from four to five, the halls were expected to be quiet. A hushed conversation could be ex-

pected to bring stern disapproval. Dormitory meetings
often centered on the problem of noise. "I've been hearing
whispers as people walk to classes," Diana said at one of
these meetings. "It's got to stop. How can we study with
all that going on?"

Diana had arrived at Bryn Mawr a Midwestern Republican, which meant she was close to being a right-wing
conservative in the eyes of most of her friends at college.
They were horrified to hear her criticize social security or
defend Richard Nixon against John Kennedy in the 1960
presidential election. Gradually, however, Diana began
to shed her Midwestern political beliefs.

The year of Kennedy's election also marked the birth
of the American student movement in Greensboro, North
Carolina, on February 1, when a small group of black college students sat down at the lunch counter of a five-and-
ten and asked to be served. The sit-in movement which
grew out of that incident spread rapidly across the upper
South and was paced by a reawakening of political concern among white students in the North. The end of the
Eisenhower era, during which the country was run like a
large corporation, with an eye always on the ledger books,
brought something like a renaissance of social awareness
to long-quiescent college campuses. The apathetic "silent generation" of the 1950s was replaced by a new generation more concerned with the *rightness* of things than
whether or not the economy was in order and the social
peace maintained. Girls who had once kept records of
the deb parties they attended and listened to Lester Lanin
records turned to Joan Baez instead. They began wearing

their hair long and their skirts short. A mild (at first) bo-
hemianism appeared on campuses where girls had once
worn stockings to class as a matter of course. Gold-rimmed
sunglasses replaced circle pins; sandals replaced loafers.
The Catcher in the Rye gave way to *Lord of the Flies*,
T. S. Eliot to Allen Ginsberg, Hollywood to the *nouvelle
vague*. It was not a time when people were inclined to admit social pretensions and Diana learned to treat lightly
the century-old name and position of her family in Dwight,
like thousands of other young people who were beginning to regard their own privileges with a critical, and
somewhat guilty, eye. Nevertheless, she defended her father's tenant farms in Likskillet, Alabama (since sold),
insisting that he, at least, treated his tenants fairly.

At home, however, she and her father both kidded
Mrs. Oughton by threatening to alter the family's listing
in the Chicago *Social Register* to read, "Mr. and Mrs.
James H. Oughton of Dwight, Illinois, and Likskillet, Alabama." Mrs. Oughton was not amused, but she accepted
Diana's new attitudes with equanimity. When Diana once
idly mentioned she no longer wanted her name included in
the *Social Register*, Mrs. Oughton began a two-year letter-
writing campaign which eventually succeeded in having
her daughter's name removed. By that time, Diana had
forgotten all about it.

Diana majored in German at Bryn Mawr and spent her
junior year at the University of Munich, living with a
Bryn Mawr friend named Karin Carlson. In the summer
of 1961 she and another Bryn Mawr friend, Linda Newman, rented a car in Paris and drove through Europe,

camping out most of the time, crossing frontiers when the mood struck them and arriving in Berlin, by coincidence, just in time to see the closing of the Brandenburg Gate as the East Germans were beginning to divide the city with a wall. Every week Diana insisted on buying lamb kidneys, which she cooked over a portable stove; she had lamb kidneys on Sunday mornings at home, she explained, and saw no reason to give them up just because she was in Europe.

Throughout her year in Europe Diana thoroughly immersed herself in German culture and life, picking up Bavarian and Swiss dialects of German along with the literary German she studied in Munich. She went to the opera often, searched secondhand book shops for early editions of Goethe, learned to enjoy idle afternoons over strong coffee, talking about nothing in particular. Blond and heavy, she began to look half German. Her fluency in the language made her sound German, too, and when her father came to visit her he found that even the Germans sometimes thought she was German. She remained erratic, however, once setting off on a trip to meet a friend in Switzerland without the note telling her in which hotel on which street in which town the meeting was to take place. (The meeting took place as scheduled; she later explained to a friend she had figured it out *logically*.) On another occasion she was excited by an account of a certain castle and made a special trip to see it. "My God!" she said when she arrived. "I've seen this castle before!"

Diana traveled constantly, worked sporadically, and spent long evenings in earnest social and political discussions with young Germans, not all of whom were grateful to America for its victory in World War II or its domination of Europe since. In one letter home she described a German boy named Peter who criticized America for the loss of its pioneer spirit, its mistreatment of women and its hostility toward socialism.

In the spring of 1962 Diana and Karin took a trip through Spain, Southern France and Italy, ending up in Rome, where Diana met some relatives she had always been close to as a child. Now they seemed provincial and insensitive. Other relatives who visited Diana in Europe struck her the same way. She described one such meeting in a letter to her parents:

> I just sat wide-eyed and listened. I didn't know people like that existed. She doesn't like anyone who hasn't a proper pedigree. Talking about poor me surrounded by all those German peasants, saying that Nuremberg was the center of world Communism. I was amazed.

Despite a quickening sense of the social inequities in the world Diana remained basically indifferent to politics. Like the rest of her generation, she awakened first to matters of style — the chrome and fins on cars, the shallowness of women's magazines, the sterility of life in the suburbs, the banality of television. Only later were these criticisms to take on political dimensions.

When Diana returned to America some of her friends found her somehow Germanized, as if she had tried, successfully, to blend into German life. That September, Diana drove to Chicago to meet Linda Newman, who had

spent the summer in Mexico. Together they drove back to
Bryn Mawr, stopping off briefly in Ann Arbor so Linda
could see a boy she knew. During the long drive they got
into an argument about William L. Shirer's *The Rise and
Fall of the Third Reich.* Diana said she had been to a lec-
ture in Germany where a professor had sharply criticized
the book for inaccuracies, especially in Shirer's account of
the killing of the Jews. Actually, Diana said conversationally, the German people never really knew what was happening and wouldn't have stood for it if they had known.
The whole thing, moreover, had been exaggerated out of
all proportion.

Linda was horrified. As a Jew herself, knowing what
happened to the Jews in Germany, she felt the concentra-
tion camps were a bloodstain on the century. How could
Diana treat the whole matter so lightly? How could she
accept an idle excuse for the murder of *six million people?*
They didn't *know?* They *ought* to have known. Diana
seemed to find it hard to understand just what it was Linda
was so upset about. You don't understand, Diana said;
this professor was an expert; he said Shirer was wrong and
he had a lot of convincing arguments behind him. Why
get so excited?

Back at Bryn Mawr Diana was still a girl who took
pleasure in almost everything she did, and was serious
about little. When she had to get up early she would wrap
an alarm clock in newspaper and place it across the room
beneath a sternly worded sign: "Get up, you bitch!" Theoretically, all the trouble of turning off the alarm would
get her up. In fact, she often slept through it anyway.

She remained vain about wearing glasses and never got used to contact lenses. Walking across the Bryn Mawr campus she would often turn to a friend beside her and, pointing to a blur, whisper, "Who's that?"

During her last year Diana joined a special tutoring program for black children with reading problems in Philadelphia's ghetto. The volunteers were only supposed to tutor one child each but Diana, horrified to discover that seventh graders could not read *at all*, soon had three. She took the train into Philadelphia two nights a week.

That same year she read John Howard Griffin's *Black Like Me*, an account of a trip made by the author through the Deep South disguised as a Negro. The widely read book marked a turning point in American attitudes toward racial problems. Coinciding with the struggle over school desegregation, Griffin's book suddenly revealed to white students that they had been living a fiction: America was not the free and democratic country which they had been taught about in school, but two nations, one of them denied all the legal rights and material advantages enjoyed by the other.

Diana's experience among black people in Philadelphia, and in Cambridge, Maryland, where she worked in a voter-registration campaign, gave her a firsthand sense of the black man's situation in America. In Philadelphia, a black friend trying to make conversation once told Diana's sister Carol, "You have such nice teeth." Diana knew that in the ghetto, where her friend lived, good teeth did not last long. She had never paid much attention to the fact that there were no Negroes at Madeira; by her last year at

Bryn Mawr she understood it was no accident there was only one Negro in her class.

Diana had only one serious boy friend during her college years, a Princeton football player named John Henrich. He was a friendly, earnest sort of young man, liked by her sisters and her parents. When he realized how much Diana hated rock music, especially on the car radio, he stopped playing it and began to learn something about classical music. When Henrich visited Dwight one fall he was eager to go pheasant shooting and Diana went with him, although without a gun, since she no longer took pleasure in killing birds. As a present, Mr. Oughton mounted a pheasant shot by Henrich. Diana went to Princeton to see him on weekends but would have nothing to do with the social life of the eating clubs, whose snobbery was legendary. She liked Henrich but she didn't love him; when he asked her to marry him, she thought it over and realized that having to think it over meant she definitely did not want to get married. Henrich, like Bryn Mawr itself, was only an interlude.

Diana was in the process of changing as her senior year at Bryn Mawr came to an end. She was like a person with a nagging religious doubt, a sense that questions of overriding moral importance exist in the world. She had begun to reject worldly values and the proprieties of society; she sensed that most people put too much importance on the trivial things and too little on the important ones; she was sensitive about her *self*, vaguely aware that privilege made one somehow unworthy. She knew that America was far larger than Dwight, that the world she had known was only the complacent veneer of American life, that important things were wrong in the country, that honesty and sincerity and moral commitment were the qualities which gave size to people and ways of life.

Diana's friends only half-noticed these changes. They all knew she had given up two nights a week to tutor black children, but it never really occurred to them that having done so ought to have revealed something fundamental about her. Some people would get married; some would go on to graduate school; Diana might well go into social work: it was as simple as that.

It was the custom at Bryn Mawr for friends to write the biographical sketches of each girl appearing in the yearbook. Diana's was written by Linda Newman, who summed her up in early 1963:

> "Das" which means that in German, goes well with her dirndl — the milkmaid from Dwight who's always on a diet — usually consisting of contact lenses . . . Traveler far and wide, but never remembers where she's been; "My God! I've seen this castle before!" A daring hitchhiker — gets in and out of trouble . . . Never studies. "I couldn't feel less like studying" . . . but can turn out a 25-page term paper in one and a half days . . . Entertains during exam week with caviar and sour cream and hearts of palm — Cartesian influence: "I don't believe you exist." Loves Bryn Mawr but has never spent a weekend here . . .

On the surface Diana seemed much the same, an open, friendly girl with a warmth and charm and liveliness that drew people to her. Diana herself did not really feel a changed person, and yet when she turned down John Henrich it was not only because he represented safety. She seemed to sense the imminence of a large experience, something indisputably important, a kind of secular calling. In Dwight her father had always expected things of her; at Bryn Mawr she had learned she was not like the rest of the girls. Their sense of themselves was not hers; she did not share their eagerness to relive their parents' lives. When she left Bryn Mawr, she left their world behind.

Delaying the Revolution

NEARLY HALF THE GIRLS in Diana's class at Bryn Mawr went on to graduate school and most of the rest married or headed for New York to begin a career. Diana did not like academic life, New York or the idea of marriage, so she joined the Voluntary International Service Assignments (VISA) program run by the American Friends Service Committee and was assigned to Guatemala. The decision was made almost idly, from a mixture of idealism, a taste for adventure and the lack of anything better to do.

During the year she spent in Europe Diana occasionally had found herself in the midst of poverty, especially in the barren Spanish countryside and along the rocky Adriatic coast of Yugoslavia, where peasants might have to clear a ton of stone to make room for a single olive tree. She had always been traveling as a tourist, however, stopping briefly and then moving on before the life of the people

lost its first picturesque glow. In the ghettos of Philadelphia, too, she had been only a visitor, staying long enough
to help children learn to read but not long enough to gain
a sense of the limits of their lives.

In the early summer of 1963 Diana was an innocent.
When she filled out her VISA application she wrote a single
word after the section marked experience: "None." The
month-long VISA training program, during which she
spent a week in New York's Spanish Harlem, and then the
two years she spent in Guatemala, gradually exposed her
to the reality of poverty, to the meanness of spirit, narrow-
mindedness and self-contempt which afflicted the poor
more than the simple lack of things.

Following a short trip to Dwight, Diana joined the
VISA training program at Pendle Hill, a Quaker retreat
outside Philadelphia, where she fell in love for the first
time. The man, D., had been seeing a friend of Diana's
from Bryn Mawr, but the friend soon left Pendle Hill for
Russia and Diana and D. began spending all their time together, sometimes disappearing for most of the day. D.
was going to India and Diana tried to switch her assignment so she could go with him, but the VISA director
denied her request. When the training session ended
Diana and D. hitchhiked together to Ann Arbor, Michigan, D.'s hometown. Diana loved D. without reservation
but there was a certain remote quality to his character.
When Diana was not allowed to switch her assignment to
India, D. said there would be no point in writing long letters for two years like lovesick teen-agers and that he, for
one, did not intend to do so. Diana, having no choice,

agreed. After saying good-by to D. at the Philadelphia airport when she left for Guatemala in August, 1963, Diana did not see or hear from him until 1965.

With a long stopover in Miami, the plane trip took nearly a full day. Diana sat next to another VISA volunteer named Mike Kimmell, a short, intelligent, caustic young man who took pride in his working-class background and Russian-Jewish ancestry. He kidded Diana about her protected upbringing and her high-mindedness in sacrificing her young womanhood to the poor Indians of Guatemala. Diana insisted that absolutely was *not* the case. She had her own reasons for going to Guatemala. By the time they arrived in Guatemala City Kimmell was half in love with her.

During her first three months in Guatemala Diana spent most of her time in the capital, Guatemala City, studying Spanish at the Guatemalan-American Institute (IGA). She and a friend from Pendle Hill, Anne Hogshead, a sensible girl who had just graduated from Mary Baldwin College in Virginia, took buses out into the countryside looking for places where they might like to work. In late September they made the rough, four-hour trip to Chichicastenango, a remote and impoverished Indian market town where the Spanish colonial and Indian cultures maintained an uneasy equilibrium.

At Pendle Hill the director of the VISA program had advised Diana to stay away from the isolated and primitive areas of Guatemala, fearing that her gentle nature and privileged background would make such a life doubly hard. In Chichicastenango Diana and Anne walked through the town, visited a convent where three Catholic priests were running a school, and asked if they could come to work. The priest who had invited them and who ran the *Caritas* missions in the province of Quiché, Father José Maria Suarez, told them they would be welcome on one condition: they must abandon any intention of teaching the Indians about birth control.

The people of Chichicastenango balanced their lives between the deeply conservative, sometimes harsh Catholicism of Spain and the ancient beliefs of their Mayan ancestors. Indians burned incense and beat drums on the steps of the large, whitewashed Catholic church which dominated the market square, while inside priests said Mass and baptized Indian children. On Thursdays and Sundays, the market days, Indians with no time for prayer would hire professionals to take their place before the images of their favorite saints. At other times the Indians would attend religious festivals in the tiny villages surrounding Chichicastenango or at secret altars in the mountains.

In Chichicastenango the priests tolerated the Indian culture and beliefs, making no effort to crush out the people's faith in *brujos*, the male witches who allegedly had magical powers to heal the sick or intervene with the ancient gods. Diana soon learned, however, that in other Guatemalan towns the Church was jealous and practiced a modern form of militant Christianity, waging relentless war against the old ways. When the Church felt itself threatened by unbelief, Diana found, it could be as cruel, in its way, as the sixteenth-century *conquistadores* who had baptized Indian children before killing them.

Life in Chichicastenango was peaceful, centering on the

market days when Indian farmers and artisans in the surrounding countryside would pack up whatever they had
to sell and carry it to town on their backs. Some of their
huge, carefully balanced loads of earthenware pots and
white wooden coffins rose six feet or more above their
heads. Whatever they failed to sell they carried home
again. The flavor of the town itself was exotic, with whitewashed Spanish colonial buildings, winding, cobblestoned
streets, gardens hidden behind high walls and massive
wooden doors, iron grillwork, the open, street-level shops
of local weavers, potters, woodworkers and other artisans.
Bells rang at matins and vespers, the smell of woodsmoke
was always in the air, everyone said good morning, good
afternoon or good evening when they met in the street.
Anne and Diana quickly settled into the quiet life of the
town.

After staying briefly at the convent they rented the
ground floor of a house that, by the standards of Chichicastenango, was a relatively sumptuous place to live. It had
a wooden floor, electricity, running water, a wood-burning
stove in the kitchen which could be used to heat water
for a shower, and an open fireplace in the living room,
all for forty dollars a month. At first work at the school
consisted largely of cooking meals for the Indian children,
but gradually they began teaching classes in Spanish, the
second language of most of the people who lived in Chichicastenango. After a while some Catholic nuns arrived
to take over the Spanish classes and Diana began teaching
adults to read while Anne, who was falling in love with a
Guatemalan doctor named Juan Aleman, began doing

office work for a clinic staffed by American doctors who had volunteered for month-long tours in Guatemala. She was often away for three or four days when the doctors made their rounds of the villages.

Diana's life also began to expand. Eventually she became the editor of a newspaper for adults just learning to read, published by the Guatemalan Army and paid for with U.S. Military Assistance funds. She also worked on a program to introduce a high-protein meal called *incaprina* to the largely undernourished Indian population. With the help of a dozen men she had taught to read in the convent school, Diana established reading classes in villages surrounding Chichicastenango, buying each of them a Coleman gas lantern in the capital, since few of the villages had electricity.

Diana was often out well after dark walking from village to village, up and down the steep *barrancos,* slash-like ravines which cut through the mountains. Absent-minded and slightly awkward, she once tumbled into a water-filled ditch in the dark. She was occasionally warned that even worse things might happen to a blonde American girl out on the roads alone at night, but she simply dismissed the warnings.

The more Diana learned about the hard life of rural Guatemala, the more she reflected on the affluence of the United States. In Chichicastenango Americans seemed an alien presence, the fact of their wealth almost an insult to the impoverished Indians. A confusion emerged in her mind that lasted the rest of her life: she had rejected affluence (at first almost unconsciously) to work among the poor, but poverty, clearly, was nothing to be envied. She hated poverty but she hated affluence, too. Transistor radios struck a jarring note in the market, and yet the Indians wanted radios, cars, sewing machines and all the other doubtful (to Diana) benefits of modern life.

When Diana and Anne had first arrived two young men with the Peace Corps were living in the town before setting up a project in an outlying village. The two came to symbolize everything Diana was learning to dislike about Americans. They lived largely like tourists, were ignorant of the language and awkward with the Indians, were self-important and insensitive, and, worst of all, were thoroughly *American*, down to their T-shirts and Coca-Cola. The Peace Corpsmen felt they were living on a level of bare subsistence with a monthly allowance of $118; Anne and Diana each received only $15, plus expense money for food and rent. The Peace Corpsmen shared a jeep and a library of technical books and seemed to be doing nothing; Diana had arrived with her clothes and almost nothing else and was working twelve hours a day.

She felt the Peace Corpsmen had needlessly cut themselves off from the Indians, especially after they bought a half-wild German shepherd puppy and then rented the entire upper floor of a house to use as a kennel. When Anne was asked to feed the dog while they were out of town on one occasion, she found the house reeking of urine and feces and the dog going blind as the result of a vitamin deficiency. Later the two young men moved into a tiny village, learned the language and worked hard on a number of projects that materially improved the lives of the villagers, but Diana's original impression never faded.

When an old school friend, Linda Newman Solomon, arrived in Guatemala City on her honeymoon that first October, Diana repeatedly mentioned the Peace Corpsmen as an example of what she did not want to be. The Solomons returned to Chichicastenango with Diana for a brief thirty-six-hour visit. They had the impression Diana was living largely on beans and invited her to join them for the excellent meals served at their hotel, the Mayan Inn. Diana sensed, but naturally did not mention, a change in her feelings for Linda, recently married and looking forward, without apparent reservations, to life as a young matron in New York. The Mayan Inn was relatively inexpensive by American standards — $22 a day — but Diana knew that was as much as an Indian family might see in six months. She was sharply conscious of the Solomons' wealth (both were heirs to considerable fortunes) and of their reluctance to eat the local foods or drink the water. "Our stomachs just wouldn't take it," Linda explained. Diana was not exactly a child of privation herself, of course, but in four weeks she had immersed herself in the life of the people and had begun to see things from their vantage point. Compared to the hardships faced by the Indians, the Solomons' life seemed shallow and overprivileged. "My God," Diana said in a kind of joking wonder to Kimmell after Linda left, "she used to be my very best friend in the whole wide world."

Gradually, Diana came to feel something close to a sense of shame at being an American. When Anne was out of town with the American clinic Diana had to do all the marketing. Tall and blond, she towered over the Indians and attracted American tourists like a beacon. She was invariably polite with them but could not help being repelled by their awkward attempts to speak Spanish, their sporty clothes, their hard bargaining for native cloth when the asking price might have represented no more than ten cents an hour for the labor involved. Diana hated to see the Indian *brujos* approach tourists with an offer to perform the ancient chicken-killing ceremony, a ritual conducted on a mountaintop altar outside the town, and she disliked the Americans even more for agreeing to pay the *brujos'* fifteen-dollar fee.

By the spring of 1964 Diana's attitude toward Guatemala had begun to take on definition. The poverty had been immediately apparent, of course, but at first it had seemed as if the country itself were poor. Gradually it became apparent that only the lower classes within the country were poor, while the upper classes were very well off indeed. There was nothing startling about the presence of rich and poor in the world, but in Guatemala Diana began to see for the first time that the rich are afraid of the poor, and that the poor hate and envy the rich.

During her first few weeks in the country she had stayed with the VISA director in Guatemala City not far from the presidential palace. Soldiers were on guard twenty-four hours a day. At that time political troubles had resulted in a strictly enforced curfew. Cars were stopped by troops at roadblocks on the city's edge and regulations required motorists to keep on their interior lights when they were driving at night. Before long Diana heard about FAR (Armed Rebel Forces), a guerrilla organization then fighting in the mountains to the east. Later, after Anne had married Juan Aleman and gone to live in Santa Cruz del Quiché, she told Diana of the time someone had painted "Viva FAR" on the wall of her house. At first she had been inclined to simply ignore it, but friends warned the police might not do the same. In the end she came out with Ajax and water and scrubbed the wall clean. Diana realized that Guatemala was a country at war.

In Chichicastenango Diana's first impressions, centering on the exotic Indian costumes and ways, quickly deepened to include a sense of the true poverty of their lives. On market days the streets were filled with thin, large-eyed children, their bellies protruding, their naturally black hair sometimes a reddish-golden color from malnutrition. Until their children were three or four years old, the Indian women nursed them, and their breasts became shriveled and flat. Once, walking in the market, Diana saw a shivering baby wrapped in newspapers lying beside an Indian woman. The baby had measles but the woman had no one to leave it with and she could not afford to miss a market day.

Old men sat in the market all day beside a load of firewood and then carried home what they had failed to sell. At the stalls of the coffin makers most of the simple wooden boxes were child-sized. Poverty hung in the air like an odor. There was little money to be seen; when a purchase was made each coin was counted out separately. The sellers of fruits or eggs or vegetables or meat never seemed to have much to sell, and the buyers chose with painful care. A woman might spend a day selling a dozen of the brown mountain eggs; another woman might go to half a dozen stalls before buying a single egg.

In Guatemala City the rich and poor eyed each other sharply; in Chichicastenango the Indians felt life had always been the same. They did not rebel, even in spirit. When they had a little money they would buy an *octava* (an eighth of a pint) of *aguardiente*, a biting, clear liquor which was a kind of national drink, or *cusha*, an illegal drink distilled from grain. A deep sadness untouched by hope was the emotion always nearest the surface in the Indians. As market days neared an end the streets would fill with drunken men and women, not brawling or shouting, but weeping. The Indians accepted their lot without questioning; they simply assumed that God was cruel. Misery hung over the town like the huge and hideous *sopilotes*, black carrion birds that waited in the trees or on rooftops for something to die, for the scraps of entrails left in the meat market, or even for the feces of dogs, horses and men.

Confronted by this misery, Diana herself embraced poverty and yet knew, with a sense of guilt, that she could escape her own poverty whenever she chose. Escape, in fact, was as close as the Mayan Inn, which was run by a Guatemalan-American but was thoroughly Spanish colonial in atmosphere. Diana found it hard to resist small physical pleasures. Anne always knew a couple of American doctors staying at the Inn and when the two girls wanted to clean up they would borrow a room for the afternoon and use the steaming hot showers and huge bath towels provided by the hotel. When they tired of the fried bananas, black beans, soup and grilled meat served at local restaurants for thirty cents, they would go to the Inn for huge meals of lamb or roast beef costing perhaps two dollars. During one period they borrowed the hotel's piano, one of the few in Chichicastenango.

Gradually, however, Diana began feeling guilty about spending so much time at the Inn. The Indian waiters, the cooks and kitchen help always in the background, the cleaning women scrubbing terraces made the town's poverty a living presence even at the Inn. On Saturday nights, when the municipal marimba band played in the Inn's huge courtyard, Indians would gather silently in the street outside the huge wooden gates. Half visible in the darkness, they stood and listened. After a while Diana began staying away from the Inn.

Diana's recognition of the poverty of Guatemala and of the half-hidden war between rich and poor led to the formation of political opinions after she met Alan Howard, a Fulbright scholar living in Guatemala City. Howard, a graduate of Hamilton College from Newton, Massachusetts, was working on an experimental reading program in the federal prison. Long conversations with political prisoners had given him a decidedly cynical view of Guatemalan politics and a sense that traditional parliamentary methods would never end the inequities which divided the country. Soft-spoken, intelligent, with a vaguely clean-cut look that belied his politics, Howard lived alone in *La Roja Zona,* the red-light district of Guatemala City. After meeting him through the IGA Diana would often spend long evenings talking about politics in Howard's austere apartment, plainly furnished but always cluttered with books and papers. Howard argued that the VISA program would never change Guatemala in fundamental ways. At best, he said, reformist programs like Diana's might help isolated individuals; at worst they would dilute the anger and desperation which alone could prompt the people to rise up and destroy the old system.

"You're only delaying the revolution," he told her.

Howard's was an old argument, but it was new to Diana. Her work in Chichicastenango seemed to confirm what he said. Sometimes she took pride in the men she had taught to read and in the classes they, in turn, had established in the outlying villages; but then she would think, so what? The country is still seventy per cent illiterate. When she talked with Guatemalans she found that many shared Howard's views: human poverty was not a fundamental thing, like poor soil or insufficient rain, but the product of a social system. Some people prospered under that system while others suffered. The only way to end the suffering was to replace the system. The idea was brutally simple, but it seemed to explain how the rich and the poor could exist side by side, and why something like war smoldered between them. Howard pointed to the experience of another American Fulbright scholar living in Guatemala. He had planned to spend a year studying the country's corporate structure but was finished almost as soon as he began: there was no corporate structure, only a handful of ruling families. A Guatemalan friend told

Diana the solution was as brutally simple as the problem. "What this country needs," he said, "is to line the fifty first families up against the white wall."

Diana was not uncritical; she saw through the radical pretensions of rich sons indulging themselves in a little fashionable rebellion. She learned the difference between genuine revolutionaries and middle-class leftists who had their eyes on the United Fruit Company. The most important factor in Diana's changing views was the simple misery of the people and her strongly emotional reaction to it. Out walking with Howard on one occasion, she stopped by a stream used by the Indians for drinking. Diana pointed to the ascarid worms in the water and began to cry. All the doctors in America might come to Guatemala, but the Indians would have to go on drinking that water. It was wrong, she felt, and when things were wrong they had to be changed. In frequent contact with Howard and others who were confident they knew *how* things ought to be changed, Diana gradually adopted their ideas. Like most people, she was not an original thinker, but she had a strong and confident mind and once she adopted an idea it became her own.

The misery of the Indians in Chichicastenango, the curfews and machine gun-carrying soldiers, the FAR rebels in the mountains to the east, the pitifully halting changes brought about by VISA, CARE, the Peace Corps and *Caritas*, the indifference of Guatemalans who could afford to eat in the Mayan Inn all seemed to confirm what Howard said.

When Diana had arrived in Guatemala she had been a

liberal, believing the only way to make a better world was
to identify the problems, and devise their solutions, one
by one. Guatemala made her into a radical: she began to
feel that things had to be changed all at once, or not at
all. Step by step, she acquired a new sense of the world
and its troubles, simple in outline but broad in its application: the name of the problem is capitalism, she concluded, and the name of the solution is socialism. She did
not acquire her faith in a flash; it was a slow conversion,
but nonetheless complete.

At the same time Diana began to feel that the United
States, too, was playing a part in the half-submerged
world struggle taking place around her. In November of
1963 Diana had been in Guatemala City when the news
of President Kennedy's assassination came over the radio.
The Americans had all been deeply shocked, depressed at
the thought a hopeful beginning in American history
might already have ended. The Guatemalans, however,
shrugged off the event as if it were of no importance. A
few even expressed a kind of vindictive pleasure, as if hop-
ing the death of their president might humble Americans.
After spending a year in Guatemala Diana began to share
their views.

During a trip to Washington in 1963 Diana and the
other VISA volunteers had spent thirty minutes with the
President's brother, Attorney General Robert Kennedy.
At the time she had been excited. Now the contrast between Chichicastenango and the power, affluence and
glamour of the Kennedys only angered her. In Guatemala
the wealth, power and complacency of the United States
seemed callous. This impression was reinforced by what

she had learned about American meddling in Guatemalan politics. She knew the Central Intelligence Agency had helped overthrow a left-wing Guatemalan government in 1954 and while she was living in Chichicastenango two CARE officials, men she had known and trusted, were accused of being CIA agents and abruptly left the country. The newspaper she helped edit was supported by U.S. Military Assistance funds, making its blandness begin to look faintly suspect.

When Howard argued that the American interest in a stable and conservative Guatemala was economic, Diana found evidence to confirm it. She knew a large gift of American baby food to CARE had been prompted by something less than charity; the manufacturer had reportedly decided distribution by CARE would introduce its product more cheaply than a country-wide advertising program. If reformism would perpetuate the status quo, then what was the purpose of the Peace Corps? Why did so much American economic aid seem to end up in the hands of the rich without affecting the lives of the poor? Why was the American military indirectly helping Guatemala to defeat the FAR guerrillas? Why did Americans — tourists, businessmen and government officials alike — seem to circulate almost exclusively in the upper classes of Guatemala? Diana's conclusions to these questions were basically two: that revolution was the only solution to injustice in Guatemala, and that the United States was actively working to prevent it from taking place.

She was never insistent about her conclusions, but she was not silent about them, either. A natural iconoclast, she often played the devil's advocate when the dozen or so VISA volunteers in Guatemala would meet in the capital to discuss projects. Behind all her arguments was the doubt that a dozen people, taking things one step at a time, could achieve anything meaningful. A dozen people might, however, form the nucleus of a revolution.

The change in Diana's thinking was immediately apparent when her family visited Guatemala during Easter week of 1964. To begin with, she wrote insisting they stay at a five-dollar-a-day hotel in Chichicastenango, not the Mayan Inn. She worried about the visit for weeks in advance, telling friends she didn't care what her family did in Guatemala City, where almost no one knew her, but that she dreaded the impression they might make in Chichicastenango. She had worked for months to create an easy relationship with the Indians she saw daily and feared that her family's obvious wealth might destroy it overnight.

Throughout the visit Diana felt a vague unease, a sense that unnamed things were beginning to separate her from her family, something deeper than the political gap which separated her from her father. Her mother, who cared and knew nothing about politics, brought Diana a suitcase full of clothes, caviar and liver pâté, most of which Diana later gave away. Diana and her father argued and joked as always but her attitude toward the poverty of Guatemala collided with his.

In Guatemala City Diana's father had long discussions about social change and revolution with Alan Howard and John Nichols, who later wrote *The Sterile Cuckoo* and other novels. Howard argued that only socialism could solve Guatemala's problems. If socialism were so effective,

Mr. Oughton pointedly wondered, why was there an Iron Curtain? Diana, Howard and Nichols were all children of the Kennedy era: talk about the Iron Curtain embarrassed them. The question was not what was best for Eastern Europe, they countered; the question was what to do about Guatemala.

Mr. Oughton found their concern for the poverty of the Indians in Chichicastenango slightly affected. The Indians were farmers, he said: why didn't VISA help them increase production? The only agricultural program Diana showed him was a demonstration rabbit-raising project. The rabbits were being fed Purina Chow. "Purina Chow!" Mr. Oughton said. "Where are the Indians going to get Purina Chow?" Diana's father was the only one who played the devil's advocate with her. Kimmell, for example, always considered himself a writer rather than a radical, but he was unwilling to challenge Diana's ideas about the processes of social change. He felt he was on her side, even if he did not agree with her on every particular. In a sense, Diana's father was the only one who took her ideas seriously. He felt revolution meant social chaos, widespread suffering and totalitarianism; he had, after all, plenty of examples of all three to which he could point. Diana felt her father's doubts were only a reflex of his age and his class. What difference could a few rabbits make? Inevitably, she felt he just didn't understand.

Despite her newly radical ideas Diana went to the trouble of obtaining an absentee ballot in the fall of 1964 so she could vote against Barry Goldwater. Her father ran for the state legislature on a blue-ribbon Republican ticket with (now) Senator Charles Percy that fall and

Diana wrote to tell him he was the only Republican for whom she had voted. Mr. Oughton answered, thanking her and pointing out in detail what scoundrels a number of the Democrats on the ticket were. The arguments between Diana and her father in Guatemala had not placed any real strain on their closeness. He kidded her about having attached herself to religious institutions despite her thoroughgoing unbelief. "You're the world's only atheist Congregationalist working for a Quaker organization under the direction of Catholic priests," he said. After her family left, Diana wrote to apologize for her snappish irritation whenever they had felt ill at ease in the strange, half-primitive surroundings of Chichicastenango. "I had forgotten how long it took me to adjust to life here," she said in the letter.

After Diana's father returned to the United States he sent her a substantial check, suggesting she use it to buy a horse for traveling through the countryside when she was checking on the progress of local reading programs. Diana, beginning to dislike buying things for herself, returned the check and suggested that her father send a similar amount to the convent school in Chichicastenango, which he did.

In spite of her growing disenchantment with the possibility of achieving meaningful, if gradual, reforms with programs like VISA, Diana continued to work at a ferocious pace, immersing herself in the life of the people and treating herself harshly. While other VISA volunteers found it difficult to live on their fifteen-dollar monthly stipend, Diana always seemed to have money left over.

There was little in her life besides work. She had a portable record player and a set of Beethoven's nine symphonies conducted by Arturo Toscanini, which she played again and again; the Second was her favorite. She read at night, exchanging paperbacks with Kimmell and Howard and asking one friend going back to America to send her a copy of Rolf Hochhuth's *The Deputy* (perhaps remembering her argument with Linda Solomon two years earlier).

When Anne left to marry Juan Aleman in July, 1964, Diana quickly moved into a much smaller apartment, not far from the market, where she lived in conditions close to those of the Indians. The floor was dirt, the walls whitewashed, the bed hard. There was no electricity or running water. She washed all her own clothes, read by candlelight and seemed to live largely on coffee and a kind of oatmeal porridge which could be prepared whenever she had a free moment. It was simpler that way. Fruit had to be soaked in a halazone solution, vegetables had to be boiled, and salad was ruled out completely. The alternative, as Anne discovered early in 1965, was amoebic dysentery, a chronic and debilitating condition that was one reason the Indians never had the energy to break out of the cycle of poverty. Diana wore Indian sandals that cost fifty cents in the market. When her clothes began to wear out she simply patched and repatched them. "Buy yourself a dress," Kimmell told her once. "No one will hold it against you." Diana insisted clothes didn't interest her.

In spite of her refusal to take the slightest advantage of her money, she retained the manners and attitudes of an aristocrat, including a contempt for bourgeois amenities and a sometimes harsh frankness which left Kimmell, who was sensitive to the proprieties, slightly scandalized. On one occasion he felt himself blush when Diana was openly delighted by the announcement of a change of assignment by a priest she didn't like. The decent thing, Kimmell felt, would have been to withhold her victorious grin until he was out of sight. Diana often offended the sensibilities of those around her and Kimmell never learned to like it.

Diana's way of life inevitably affected her health. She lost weight and suffered asthma attacks, the first of her life. When the first attack occurred she refused to leave Chichicastenango, instead retreating into bed, against all advice, to wait it out. Anne came and took care of her, keeping the fire going around the clock to help dry out the air. Lying there in the gloom, Diana told Anne about D. and said she sometimes wished they had never promised not to write each other. She had written him twice, she said, but had received no reply in return. "The only time I feel blue is when I'm sick," she told Anne, trying to explain her mood. Later, referring to D. again, she said, "I wish I had enough nerve to just go ahead and have a baby." She never mentioned D. again.

Diana embraced the poverty of the Indians in Chichicastenango and mastered a fluent, idiomatic Spanish which allowed her to move among them freely. At the same time, however, she ignored and even flouted many of the Indians' most deeply held convictions about how people ought to behave. At the convent Diana taught English to Father Laureano Gonzalez, ignoring the whispers caused by the hours they spent alone together. On one occasion, during a visit to another town, Diana and two other girls stripped off their clothes and went swimming not far from a scandalized Guatemalan gardener and in sight of the house where they were staying. She ignored the helpful warnings of Indians who said it was not only dangerous, but improper, for young women to go trooping around the countryside in the dark. She was only amused when some Guatemalans mistook her for a prostitute because she and Anne were out walking well after proper Guatemalan girls were expected to be at home. When she took the bus into Guatemala City she would offer cigarettes to the Indian men sitting around her, ignoring their astonishment at her boldness.

In the convent one afternoon Father José Maria Casas invited Anne and Diana to join him in a game of target shooting in the courtyard. Anne, who had never fired a rifle, failed to hit anything, but Diana surprised them both by never missing. After that Father Casas always called her *Diana La Cazadora*, Diana the Huntress.

The priests had decidedly mixed feelings about Diana. They respected her dedication but considered her to be unfeminine, by which they meant large and confident rather than demure, delicate and retiring. They criticized her for lacking *amor proprio*, meaning something more like self-regard than self-love. They felt Diana wrongly abused herself by dressing, eating and sleeping badly, and by working *all* the time. They felt she lacked the requisite degree of pride, self-esteem and dignity.

In return, Diana had mixed feelings about the priests. She respected their lack of worldly ambition and their lifelong commitment to the Indians, but was disturbed by their comfortable, almost complacent way of life. Their vows of poverty were flexible enough, she noted, to include an excellent Indian cook named Diego, soft beds and large rooms, cars and record players and wine with meals. She was disturbed by their calm acceptance of suffering. The conservative cast of their Catholicism angered her. She vaguely suspected them of acquiescing in the status quo, as if they had been reconciled to the idea that charity and people in need of charity were both part of God's eternal order. The priests, of course, could view the present from the perspective of Christian history. They felt their efforts were only the most recent in two thousand years of human suffering and attempts to relieve that suffering. If they did not change things overnight, they were not much surprised. Diana lacked their patience. Sacrificing everything in this world and doubting there was another, Diana wanted to see some results now. She felt that no matter how hard she and the priests worked, there would always be more people than food or jobs or places to live.

Toward the end of her last year she got into a dispute with one of the priests after bringing the subject of evolution into one of her adult reading classes. "Father Casas is one of the finest men I've ever met," she told Kimmell, "but he's a fool, too." If the priests still balked at evolution, how could they ever hope to bring the Indians of Chichicastenango into the modern world? Diana respected their admirable human qualities but refused to believe their approach could be the answer.

The longer Diana remained in Chichicastenango, the

more she felt that the priests were an integral part of the system, the smiling face which hid a social order's grim determination to keep what it had. Doubting the value of what she was doing, Diana redoubled her efforts. Her life was her work, broken only by long conversations with Kimmell and Howard whenever she got away from Chichicastenango. In the town she did whatever had to be done. When two local Indian children began going blind with an eye disease which demanded an operation possible only in the capital, Diana spent weeks prodding the sluggish Guatemalan bureaucracy, taking the two children into the city a number of times and returning the same day. The situation was typical of Guatemala. Because Diana refused to let the matter slide, the sight of these two Indian children was saved; but hundreds of others throughout the country went blind.

Shortly before leaving Guatemala in the summer of 1965 Diana wrote home to her parents in an attempt to explain what the two years in Chichicastenango meant to her:

> When you work at such a basic level with people from a different culture, with different values and different ways of thinking, you really have to seek a common denominator of understanding. Instead of talking about the equality of the races, you live with it, get past the hump that many people get stuck on and begin to really look at people as people with needs, happinesses, tragedy. I have to admit grudgingly that I benefited far more than the inhabitants of "Chichi" from these two years. I've come to a real understanding of that which one might call an ideal, practically gained.

She did not mention her long conversations with Howard or her gradually changing ideas about the world, her country, and the background of her life. When an Aid for International Development (AID) official, impressed by her fluency in Spanish, offered her a job she was flattered but refused to consider the offer seriously. She no longer believed that American and Guatemalan interests could be reconciled. She felt that working for AID would inevitably put her on the side of the Guatemalan ruling classes, who resisted change. At the same time, she had developed a hunger for simplicity. Never particularly vain or possessive, she had acquired a kind of moral horror at vanity and affluence in a world where so many still had so little.

She remembered the priests at the convent with real affection and carried their letters with her until the week she died, but she no longer believed in what they were doing. She felt it was senseless to help the victims of a cruel system when the system itself might be changed. In such circumstances, helping the victims was itself a kind of cruelty. In an abstract way Diana felt that revolution was the answer to Guatemala's problems, but that conclusion told her nothing about how *she* ought to live in the United States. She had lost her old conception of herself, but had not yet replaced it with a new one. She returned to America disillusioned, but still unformed.

Children Are
Only Newer People

BACK IN THE UNITED STATES Diana's old friends noticed that she had been somehow touched by the poverty she had seen in Guatemala, both saddened and matured, but they found her otherwise unchanged. She went home to Dwight with D., who had returned from India, but only stayed briefly. Diana's father found D. decidedly strange and wondered how Diana managed to put up with his short-tempered melancholy. Diana herself seemed quieter and sadder than she had been as a schoolgirl, nervous in the large, comfortable house on South Street in Dwight, restless through the slow summer days when the downtown streets were empty and the heat rose off the surrounding fields in heavy, shimmering waves. Mr. Oughton was concerned but not really worried by his daughter's mood; after two years of living in the almost primitive conditions of rural Guatemala it was only natural she would need a month or two to readjust to American life.

Diana's sister Carol was eager to like D. but found him cold and pretentious. Once she asked conversationally if he had stopped off in Europe on his way back from India. "There is nothing in Europe that would interest me," he said.

Before long Diana and D. went back to Philadelphia.

That summer Diana helped organize an American tour for the children's choir from the convent school in Chichicastenango. When the choir appeared in New York Diana came up from Philadelphia and stayed with the Solomons. The first night she insisted on preparing a sumptuous meal of soft-shelled crabs, which she knew Linda's husband Peter especially liked. Linda remembered the lamb kidneys Diana had insisted on cooking every Sunday morning during the summer they spent traveling through Europe. Soft-shelled crabs seemed entirely in character.

That weekend Diana accompanied the Solomons to the pre-Revolutionary house they were restoring near Stamford, Connecticut, where she spent most of a day stripping the paint from a door. Diana always liked to keep busy, and loved a project, Linda remembered. She sensed no strain between them, but did not see Diana again for three years.

In Philadelphia Diana moved into the faintly bohemian area of Powelton Village, looked around for something to do and went out with D. at irregular intervals. Their relationship never relaxed or ripened; D. insisted that she call or come to see him only at certain hours. Diana's old roommate in Germany, Karin Carlson, spent a weekend in Philadelphia and found her tense and unhappy.

When Karin said she was looking forward to meeting D. Diana was vague, alluding to the rules which governed their relationship and then changing the subject. Her apartment seemed to reflect her mood; it was Spartan and bare. The cupboard contained only canned delicacies like palm hearts, caviar, smoked oysters and backs of lamb, sent by her mother. Karin made a dinner of sorts from the lamb. She assumed that D.'s odd behavior explained Diana's low spirits and indecision.

Like Linda Solomon, Karin was bustling ahead with her own life and felt Diana would soon be doing the same. That fall Diana went out to Bryn Mawr to see her former German professor, Christoph Schweitzer, who was struck by her feeling for the poverty of the Guatemalan Indians. On Thanksgiving Diana had dinner with Mike Kimmell. Generally, however, she saw few people in Philadelphia, as if waiting until she regained a sense of herself.

She got a job in the Museum of Art's gift shop but quit after two and a half days to take a teaching job with an adult reading program funded by the Office of Economic Opportunity (OEO). After Guatemala the heavily bureaucratic OEO program was a disappointment. She was irritated by the other teachers, who seemed interested mainly in picking up a quick $100 a week, and even to some degree by the ambitious, thoroughly middle-class Italians enrolled in the program. After $15 a month in Guatemala the $100 a week she earned in Philadelphia seemed a fortune; the money vaguely troubled her. She wanted to do things for other people, but she hated the idea that helping people could be turned into a successful career. When D. returned to Ann Arbor, Michigan, late in 1965, Diana decided to go with him. In January, 1966, she enrolled in a Master of Arts program at the University of Michigan's School of Education. Not long after, Diana's relationship with D., such as it was, came to an end.

When Diana entered the University of Michigan it was still a Midwestern school where students were inclined to be serious about football, fraternities, weekends and the drinking of beer. The Students for a Democratic Society (SDS) had been largely created by two University of Michigan students, Al Haber and Tom Hayden, in June, 1962, and the first teach-in on Vietnam had been held at the University of Michigan in March, 1965, but radicalism had remained an elite, intellectual pastime. Combined with an old student political party called Voice, SDS at Michigan was closer to being a study group than a genuine political organization.

The vast majority of students spent their time worrying about graduate schools, careers and how to stay out of the Army.

Ann Arbor itself was comfortable and prosperous, with tree-lined streets and large brick and frame houses built in the early part of the century. It was cold and snowy during the long winters, rainy in the fall and spring. Undergraduate girls still had to sign out on weekends and obey parietal hours, and the undergraduate boys were still more likely to wear loafers and button-down shirts than blue jeans or boots. The war in Vietnam, the drug revolution already beginning in San Francisco, the shift in taste from folk music to acid rock had not yet arrived in

Michigan. Detroit, about forty minutes away by car, had one of the first of the underground newspapers, the *Fifth Estate*, but its troubled voice did not find many listeners in Ann Arbor.

Diana made friends with some people in Voice-SDS and told them about her experiences in Guatemala. That summer she returned to Guatemala and stayed briefly with the new director of the program there, Bill Dreyer. She told Bill's wife Donna she had been working for the OEO in Philadelphia and Donna kidded her about working for the federal government. "You, of all people," she said. During that visit, with Alan Howard's help, Diana arranged to meet with some leaders of FAR, which had moved into Guatemala City and was raising money to continue its revolutionary efforts by kidnaping the wives or children of bankers, doctors, lawyers and other members of the aristocratic and professional classes. Diana vaguely felt that a relationship between American radicals and Guatemalan revolutionaries might be useful. The meeting was held in deep secrecy but nothing came of it.

In September, 1966, Diana began teaching part-time at Ann Arbor's year-old Children's Community School (CCS), which occupied two basement rooms of the Friends Center on Hill Street. The school, established the previous fall by a woman named Toby Hendon, was based on the permissive principles developed by A. S. Neill at Summerhill. Children were allowed to do what they liked when they liked, on the premise that both teaching and learning were most successful when most spontaneous. Neill had concluded that humans were violent and competitive because of the way they were educated. If they were brought up to pursue things for their own sake, and were treated with understanding and love from the beginning, violent impulses would never have a chance to take root in their personalities. The Children's Community School, run largely by college students who felt their own educations had been dismal failures, pursued Neill's principles with a vengeance.

Also teaching at the school that fall were Sue Whitney, Milton Taube (known as Skip) and Bill Ayers, a blond-haired, easygoing young man with a taste for politics and women. It was sometimes hard to know which came first with him. When Ayers had arrived at the University of Michigan he had followed his older brother, Tim, into Beta Theta Phi, a fraternity known for its athletes and Saturday night parties; but he had quickly tired of football games followed by beer and pretzels.

Ayers began to take an interest in protest politics after President Johnson escalated the war in Vietnam during 1965.

On Friday, October 15 of that year, Ayers, a well-known Ann Arbor radical named Eric Chester, and twenty-six other Michigan students were arrested during a sit-in held in the Ann Arbor draft board. As Ayers' politics had moved steadily to the left his relationship with his father, chairman of the Commonwealth Edison Company of Chicago and a trustee of Northwestern University, had steadily worsened. He received a substantial allowance from home but held his father in a kind of contempt for providing it. "If he wants to finance the revolution that's okay with me," he told a friend a couple of years later. In the fall of 1966, when he and Diana first met, Ayers was boyish, articulate, good-looking and passionately interested in progressive education, not yet a revolutionary but already experienced in captivating girls with a combination of charm and social anger. Drawn to each other by their common commitment to children, spending entire days together at the Children's Community School, both rebelling against privileged backgrounds and considering themselves radicals, Diana and Bill fell in love and eventually moved into an attic room in a house on McKinley Street rented by Nancy Frappier, whose daughter René was in the first grade at the Community School.

Progressive principles at CCS did not end with allowing children to proceed at their own pace in subjects of their own choosing. The school also tried to establish complete equality between white and black students and to involve parents in the running of the school, so that it might be a community in the largest sense of the word. At first Diana held a number of odd jobs, went to school and worked at CCS whenever she could, but gradually she spent more and more of her time with the children and with Bill. At the University of Michigan she was known only as "Bill's girl." She was always vague about her background, once telling an acquaintance who asked what her father did, "Oh, he's a farmer." In January, 1967, a girl who had known Diana at Madeira years before wrote a mutual friend to say she had met:

> Dos Oughton, who is, unexpectedly, doing part-time drudge typing down the hall from my office in the linguistics department, a very swinging place lemme tellya, houris drifting in and out at all hours; she is taking a masters in education or something and working three

mornings a week or something. She is thinner than she was but she still walks funny and she never combs her hair.

Later that year Diana dropped almost everything else and began working at the school full-time, spending evenings and weekends with the children and their families. The total absorption of Bill, Skip and Diana in the school eventually made Sue Whitney feel faintly guilty about wanting a private life with her husband. The only one of the four with a regular teaching degree, she quit to teach elsewhere.

Early in 1967 Diana's sister Carol, who was living in Washington, wrote to say that the radical journalist I. F. Stone was looking for an editorial assistant fluent in Spanish to help put out his *Weekly*. Did Diana want the job? Diana thought about the offer for several months. The job itself was just the kind of thing she would like to do and her own politics at that time were close to Stone's. At the same time she was deeply involved in running the Community School and was in love with Bill. In the end she decided to stay in Ann Arbor.

Her relationship with her family was becoming increasingly strained, especially whenever her father tried to persuade her to take up a more sensible way of life. Diana's mother never understood her daughter's behavior at all; she expected girls to dress well and marry and entertain, not pursue careers which did not even have the virtue of providing a decent living. She was embarrassed by Diana's boots and jeans and too-often unwashed hair and did not really know how to explain her to friends.

Partly as a result of this atmosphere of unfocused disapproval Diana did not often return to Dwight. When her father tried to give her an allowance in March, 1967, she wrote to say:

> I don't want you to give me an allowance. It's important to me to be on my own, to feel I can support myself, to have responsibility for my own life. I feel like this, and I'm asking you to respect it. I think by age 25 I have the right to live the way I want, without feeling guilty that my way of life upsets you.

About a year later Diana's father created a family-owned corporation to operate his corn and soybean land. Diana took a few days off from the school to go back to Dwight for the signing of papers; thereafter she received quarterly dividend checks. Mr. Oughton had hoped the new arrangement would strengthen Diana's ties to Dwight but it failed to do so; in the following years he often did not know where to send her checks.

The two years Diana worked at the school were among the happiest of her life. She and Bill believed in the school and established an extraordinarily close relationship with the students. They spent weekends and holidays together. They felt they were a part of a new generation which was going to revitalize America. Diana talked about Bill with anyone who would listen, telling her family what he had said about this or that. Like Bill, she dressed in a rough style halfway between woodsmen and the working class — boots, jeans, woolen shirts, leather coats. When Bill began wearing wire-rimmed glasses she did, too. Her life centered on his. When he began serving a thirty-day jail sentence in late 1967, more than two years after his arrest in the October, 1965, draft board sit-in, Diana wrote him regularly and prepared for Christmas, when he was to get out. On a shopping trip in Chicago she carried around a letter addressed to Bill in the Washtenaw County Jail and ostentatiously put it down on store counters whenever she wrote a check. She bought him a pair of leather pants and he managed to find her a long print dress from India.

As an experiment, however, the school had mixed results. The children learned a lot of things they never would have learned in the Burns Park Elementary School, but they made almost no progress in reading, writing and arithmetic. Education at CCS was haphazard in the extreme. On one occasion one of the students wondered what a dead man looked like and the whole school trooped over to the city morgue to see one. The student who had expressed the original interest was fascinated, but some of the other children were upset. One day they might learn something about the sexual life of flowers and the next something about cowboys and Indians, but the lessons never seemed to add up to anything.

Like Diana, Bill was totally committed to the school. He had an infectious enthusiasm for whatever he did, an astonishing rapport with children, an ability to improvise brilliantly (if irregularly) as a teacher. On one occasion he brought a car battery to school and held the entire group of students spellbound while he led a discussion from the battery to electronics, physics, the universe and beyond. At the same time he was somewhat unreliable: parents and academic sponsors from the School of Education were never quite certain his interest would maintain itself.

More important than the academic chaos were the subtle racial tensions which began to emerge. Bill and Diana refused to interfere in disputes between students, and in fights the black children tended to get the best of the white children. One father withdrew his son, saying, "They're turning him into a racist." Bill and Diana felt the only way white and black children could grow up free of racial animosity was to allow them to treat each other completely as equals, which included allowing them to fight if they felt like it. Eventually, the theory went, they would learn to live together. The parents of some of the white children felt the situation was in fact a one-way street. Black parents were not happy about the situation, either. One reason they were sending their children to CCS was to keep them out of fights. They had, in fact, largely misunderstood the purpose of the school. They had hoped it would be an elite institution which would help their children to get into good colleges so they would be able to find good jobs. Bill and Diana, inclined to feel there *were* no good jobs in America, saw the school as a first step in building a new America where people would be less prejudiced, competitive and acquisitive. Their indifference to clothes, manners and traditional academic subjects was in sharp conflict with the upward-striving, highly class-conscious black parents who wanted to rise in American society, not remake it.

The single most important failing of the school, and the one on which it foundered in the end, was the fact that no one ever learned to read there. Bill and Diana always assumed the children would ask someone to teach them to read as soon as they really wanted to learn to read, but in the three years of the school's life that time never seemed to arrive. The explanation was fairly simple: the school was too rowdy for anything as organized and time-consuming as reading. The school's two rooms were divided into a "noisy" room where students could do as they pleased and a "quiet" room where, theoretically, they could do things like draw, talk to Bill and Diana, or, if the mood struck them, start learning to read. In practice, both rooms were generally chaotic with shouting, running children who often spilled upstairs into the rest of the Friends Center.

Diana's attitude toward formal education was made clear one night in the fall of 1967 when Mr. Oughton took her and Bill to dinner after a visit to the school. Always ready for a debate, Mr. Oughton was critical of the premises behind the school. He argued that permissive education was fine until you tried to teach children things like the alphabet. Diana wondered if learning the alphabet was really all that important. Her father said he had known secretaries who did not know the alphabet, the result being documents filed into permanent oblivion. Diana was not impressed. She felt things were *profoundly* wrong with America and that one of those things was excessive worry about irrelevant matters like the sequence of letters.

Arguments based on the complexity of modern industrial society had little effect on Bill and Diana; as far as they were concerned it would be okay if the entire society collapsed the following morning. This was not simply flippancy, but rather a sense that the details of political problems presented a kind of trap. To allow oneself to be forced into prescribing exact solutions was to lose the initiative which came with the attack. They wanted to create a school in which children would be loving and unafraid, not tense, competitive and obedient like the children in Burns Park Elementary School. They wanted to prepare children for the new America, not for the job scramble in the old America. If they failed to learn to read until they were ten or fifteen, well, so be it. This attitude, never articulated into a principle of the school, exactly, but always in the background of the way it was run, was resented by the parents of a number of the children, and especially by the black parents.

The reading problem reached a kind of crisis when children began to ask their parents to teach them to read. The first was Nancy Frappier's daughter René, who said she wanted to go to Burns Park for a year. Knowing how seriously her mother took CCS, René promised she would go back to Bill and Diana after she had learned to read. At about the same time Lidie Howes's daughter, Marjorie, asked her mother to teach her to read at home in the evenings.

"Why don't you ask Bill or Diana to teach you?" Mrs. Howes asked.

"That's not the kind of thing you do there," Marjorie said.

Like René, Marjorie was always polite about the school

because she knew her mother and father believed strongly in what it was trying to accomplish. In truth, however, she did not really like going there. She liked and trusted Bill and Diana, but tired of the constant shouting and roughhousing. Often she would simply leave after an hour or so, walking home in mid-morning with her younger brother Timothy, and sometimes with five or six other children, too.

Bill, Diana and Skip Taube spent a long evening at the Howes' discussing the problem. Alan Howes, a professor of English at the University of Michigan, made it clear he was sympathetic to the aims of the school but that he wanted his daughter to be able to read, too. Diana was adamant: children should not be pushed into reading under any circumstances. Bill was not quite so rigid. "It's all right to give them a little push when they're really ready," he said. The group finally decided to set up a kind of quiet hour for reading every afternoon, but within a few days the natural chaos at the school reasserted itself and the reading problem was never resolved.

In the fall of 1967 Bill was appointed director of the school, but he found himself powerless to halt the school's steady drift toward a double crisis caused by a chronic shortage of funds and the withdrawal of children by disappointed parents. Early in 1968 he announced he would probably leave the school at the end of that academic year to work full-time with SDS, but he continued the effort to solve the school's problems. Diana went on a local radio station to appeal for contributions and designed a fund-raising button with a smiling face and the legend, CHILDREN ARE ONLY NEWER PEOPLE. A bucket drive by University of Michigan volunteers was also organized, but it failed to solve the school's financial problems. On one occasion while Bill was soliciting funds on the University of Michigan campus a woman huffed by saying she would *never* contribute to that Communist institution. Bill shrugged off the incident. "I don't care what kind of reaction I get," he said with a grin. "I just like to get a reaction."

While the school's problems were mounting Bill decided to run for election to the Ann Arbor school board on a platform of educational reform. Running with him was Joan Adams, a black member of the school's board of directors and mother of one of the children at CCS. Both were supported in militant broadsides by the Radical Education Project (REP), an Ann Arbor organization of long standing which was loosely affiliated with SDS. In his public appearances Ayers was uncompromisingly radical. When he and Mrs. Adams were both soundly defeated, she felt, with some justice, that it was partly his fault.

Adding to the school's financial problems was a request by the Friends Center that it move out by the fall of 1968. The Friends said they were sorry, but pointed to the heavy physical damage left by two years of rampaging children. The other locations considered by the school all would have demanded substantial sums of money to meet zoning and state education codes, so the school decided to apply for funds to the Washtenaw County board of the Office of Economic Opportunity in Ann Arbor. When the board met to consider the application in June, 1968, the most determined opposition seemed to come from black members of the community, including some who had children at the school. They argued that the money could be better spent on other programs with a potential for concrete achievement, and that the Children's Community School was not helping children to get ahead in life.

One of the arguments made during the debate was that Bill and Diana were unfit to teach children because they were living together even though they were not married. The attack was completely unexpected and came as a shock to Bill and Diana, who had never really considered that hostility toward the school might also be directed at them. They were less angry than hurt, as if they had been personally rejected despite the two years of unending effort they had put into making the school work. The biggest disappointment came when Joan Adams, chairman of the OEO board, abstained in the voting on the school's application at a moment when she might have broken a 5-5 tie. Later another board member voted against the grant and it was rejected. There was never an open break with Mrs. Adams or the other people who spoke out against the school, but the disappointment was bitter and deep. After the meeting Skip Taube seemed to speak for all of them when he said, "I've always thought you could live without hating people, but you can't."

Later that summer OEO officials at a higher level offered a grant to the school outside normal channels, but only if certain conditions were met. Bill, realizing that his original aims were now out of the question, rejected the offer, and the school folded before the fall term would

have begun in September. The closing of the school hit
Diana harder than it did Bill. Teaching meant more to
her and she had always been more willing to compromise
to keep the school open. During that spring she had begun losing weight again. "You're losing your butt," Mrs.
Adams used to kid her. "Those hip-huggers aren't huggin'
too much." Since girlhood Diana had had long blond
hair. At the school children had teased her by pretending
they would cut it when she wasn't looking. After the
school closed Diana cut her hair, leaving barely enough
to cover her ears. It left her looking cold and severe.

Diana's two years with the school ended on a bitter
note, partly because of the official harassment which had
plagued the school from the beginning, but more impor-
tantly because of the rejection of the school by blacks. In
its essence the conflict had been a simple one: Bill and
Diana were committed to helping the black children, but
rejected the terms on which the black parents wanted their
children to be helped.

Later Bill and Diana would tend to blame the school's
failure on the various public officials who had harried it
by insisting on the letter of laws which did not seem to be
enforced so strictly elsewhere. In fact, however, the school
failed because parents were withdrawing their children.

Bill and Diana had been correct in thinking that American education suffered a host of failings, and had been
encouraged in their experiments by educational experts
who felt their work had value, but in the end it was clear
that a gulf separated them from those they most wanted
to help. The same dilemma which Diana had found in

Guatemala reappeared at the Children's Community School. She rejected a system which denied its benefits to some of its citizens, but at the same time refused to admit the alleged benefits were truly worth having. Thus she was always most opposed to those she most wanted to help, since they were the most eager for the things she most detested.

It was a bitterly frustrating experience, but Diana and Bill were naturally unwilling to focus their bitterness on blacks who wanted their children to get ahead in life, or on parents who wanted their children to read, or on the children themselves. Instead they focused it on *the system,* those interlocking strands of American society which had created things as they were, and which had to be torn apart if that society were ever to be reconstructed after a different pattern. In this way Bill and Diana, like thousands of other young Americans, came to believe the oppressed could be saved only in spite of themselves, since part of their oppression lay in their desire to become like their oppressors. The oppressed were to be encouraged to struggle, but not to be allowed to decide what they were struggling for.

Even before the Children's Community School died Bill and Diana had been growing increasingly active in SDS. After Nancy Frappier's daughter left the school Bill and Diana moved into a house of their own on Felch Street which gradually turned into a kind of commune with a shifting population of young activists and radicals.

In March, 1968, Diana helped create a women's liberation group at a time when the issue was only just begin-

CHILDREN ARE ONLY NEWER PEOPLE   73

ning to emerge among radicals around the country. The group used to meet every week or so wherever it could find room. Diana urged Doris Cummings, the mother of one of the children at CCS, to attend the meetings, and she became the only black woman who ever joined the group. Most of the talk seemed to center on the subordinate role of women in the radical movement and on the sexual oppression of women by the "macho" tendency of males to think of sex as conquest. Diana would sit on the floor, wearing boots and pants, biting her lip when she was thinking and then, when she was trying to explain something, touching the tips of her fingers to her thumb, one after the other, as if ticking off the points of what she had to say. She often talked about the role of women in SDS, which seemed to consider women a convenient mixture of sexual object, housemaid and office clerk. Why should women have to do all the typing and make all the coffee while the men decide on lofty matters of ideology and strategy? Diana insisted she was not the housemaid of the Felch Street commune. "Bill's got to do the laundry, too," she said.

In fact, however, Bill did not do the laundry, or anything else. After a couple of months of keeping things going Diana finally put her foot down and said everyone would have to help or the house would go uncleaned. The house went uncleaned. Eventually it became something a little short of a genuine health hazard.

At another meeting of the women's group Diana insisted that she and Bill were both equally free in sexual matters. They liked each other, of course, but if they felt like an adventure on the side that was okay, too. Bill's reputation as a ladies' man (he had even approached the mothers of children at the Community School) made Doris wonder if Diana was really being honest about the way this principle operated in practice.

"Are you sure this is going to work both ways?" she asked.

"You asked me that before," Diana snapped, irritated by Doris's skepticism.

"I know," said Doris, "but I'm asking you again."

"Yes, I'm sure," Diana said.

Later that year, however, Diana told another friend about a time when she had left Ann Arbor for five days. When she got back Bill calmly told her he had slept with a different girl every day she had been gone. Diana told the friend she tried to convince herself it didn't matter, but that the thought hurt anyhow.

Diana's growing involvement with women's liberation, the SDS and radical student politics widened the gap between herself and her old friends from Bryn Mawr, most of them living comfortable upper-middle-class lives while Diana was spending the majority of her time with people at least three or four years younger than she was. The last time she had seen most of her Bryn Mawr friends was in March, 1968, when Karin Carlson married Merrill Rosenberg in Chicago. At a dinner party the night before the wedding Diana got into a long political argument with Herb Erfurth, a friend of Karin's. The next day Diana changed before the wedding ceremony at the home of another Bryn Mawr girl, where she met Linda Solomon for the first time since the summer of 1965. Linda, still nursing her first child, a three-month-old boy, had flown to Chicago that morning and would be leaving in the evening. Alone together as they changed, the two girls found they had almost nothing to say to each other. Diana was wearing corduroy jeans, boots, and a brown suede jacket, and was carrying an old suitcase filled with unclean clothes piled in on top of each other. Linda was neat and organized, every inch a well-to-do woman of responsibility.

"Look at this," Diana said, taking a white dress out of her suitcase. "My mother insisted on buying it. I'd never buy anything like this myself. It cost twenty-six dollars." She affected to be stunned at the price. Linda, who thought nothing of buying twenty-six-dollar dresses, did not know what to say. Diana, who had stopped wearing a bra months before, made a special point of putting one on for the wedding.

After the ceremony and the reception Diana and Linda went back to the same house and again changed together. Linda was flying back to New York and offered to take Diana to Chicago's O'Hare Airport, a long taxi ride from the house where they were changing. Diana said fine. The awkwardness between them persisted as the cab moved through the darkening streets, then entered the expressway. Linda couldn't understand why they could not speak to each other. Suddenly she asked, "Dos, what's happened to us? Why are we so far apart?"

They began to talk but everything they said only increased the distance between them. Diana said she was living in a commune with Bill, describing him as an absolutely *terrific* person, and added that they were trying to have a baby. In fact, Diana said, she thought she was already pregnant. Linda asked if they were planning to get married. Diana scoffed at the idea. How could anyone do anything so thoroughly conventional and bourgeois and *limiting* as get married? She never planned to marry. Linda sensed there was something exaggerated in Diana's insistence on everything, but every time she tried to reestablish the warmth which had once existed between them, Diana seemed to withdraw. She was harsh and unyielding, as if all those things Linda accepted so easily in the course of life in fact presented sharp moral issues of the first importance.

At the airport Linda paid for the cab. Diana, who was flying back to Detroit, told Linda she had a youth card so she would have to pay only half fare. "Have you got one?" she asked.

"A youth card?" Linda said. "Dos, I'm twenty-eight years old. I'm a mother. What would I be doing with a youth card?"

They said good-by and never saw each other again.

The Jesse James Gang

THE RUSH OF POLITICS swept up Diana and Bill Ayers in 1968 and they almost ceased to lead personal lives. Long associated with Voice-SDS in Ann Arbor in a casual sort of way, they found themselves in the front ranks of national SDS by the end of the year. Radical politics is a heady mixture of idealism and intrigue. Cut off from most institutional sources of power, radical organizations depend entirely on ideological constituencies. They can flower, or wither, overnight.

For fifteen months in 1968 and 1969, SDS was at the precarious head of the American student movement, a small group of young men and women, with their own purposes, speaking for hundreds of thousands. During that brief period SDS grew from a band of democratic idealists into the ideological nucleus of a revolutionary party, unsteady with dreams of power. If the hundreds of thousands changed with them, they would alter the course of history.

The SDS which Bill and Diana had known at Ann Arbor was a small group with large theories for the remaking of America. It was a debating society with evangelical aims, committed to the old SDS slogan, "A free university in a free society." Instead of salvation, it promised a social utopia. Instead of God, it worshiped The People. Intellectually, it was exciting in the same way that the table talk of Jesuits is exciting, but, as an organization, SDS resembled the Society of Jesus in the secular twentieth century, not the militant Jesuit soldiers for Christ who helped conquer the New World and intrigued in the courts of Europe in the sixteenth and seventeenth centuries. Bill and Diana had the zeal of Jesuits, and they had the ancient Jesuits' harsh conviction that people did not have the moral right to be wrong on ultimate questions.

By the middle of 1968, after three years of bloody war in Vietnam, the misty idealism of the early student movement, and of Bill and Diana before the closing of the Children's Community School, had begun to harden. They were beginning to sense the realities of power and they were tired of being its victims. The early student movement had borrowed its principal moral stance from Albert Camus, who insisted that thinking men had to find a way in the modern world to be neither victims nor executioners. Having been the victims in a thousand battles with the police, student radicals began to see themselves as executioners.

Four major events transformed the American student movement in 1968, turning activists into self-proclaimed

Marxist-Leninist revolutionaries. In chronological order, those events were the Vietcong's Tet offensive in January and February; the insurrection at Columbia University in April; the near-revolution in France in May; and the Democratic Convention in Chicago in August. Each of those events helped change the terms in which American radicals thought about their own situation. The Tet offensive dramatically ended the image of Vietnamese as the helpless victims of American power; the uprising at Columbia showed that resolute action could win overnight what patient organizing might fail to achieve in months; the May revolution in France proved that Western countries could be overthrown; the Democratic convention seemed a sign that the American system was breaking down. At the beginning of 1968 Bill and Diana had assumed, like the vast majority of the radical movement, that American stability precluded any possibility of a genuine revolution. By the end of the year the country seemed bitterly divided and morally bankrupt. With the right kind of push, they felt, anything might happen. They were tired of waiting and they no longer had the slightest allegiance to democracy as they found it in America.

In its early years SDS had been concerned with questions of political morality. By the end of 1968 it was obsessed by the moral crimes of Vietnam; they felt anything was justified if it might end that crime and prevent its repetition. To do this, SDS felt a revolution was needed; the only question which preoccupied them was how to bring it about.

Bill and Diana were introduced to the excitement of national SDS in June, 1968, when they attended the annual convention held at Michigan State University (MSU) in East Lansing. Their companion and sponsor was Eric Chester, a leader of Voice-SDS in Ann Arbor and an occasional resident of the Felch Street commune. During the six-day convention (June 9-15) Bill and Diana were suddenly plunged into the passionate politics of a national student organization, dull plenary sessions where delegates dozed through the reading of interminable position papers, followed by intrigue, parliamentary maneuvering, caucusing in the corridors and late-night discussions. It was immediately apparent to Bill and Diana that they were on the side of the so-called *New Left* faction of SDS, opposed by the Progressive Labor Party faction.

The New Left had no coherent ideology but was inclined toward a passionate radicalism which combined a belief in community and a mystical faith in The People with a taste for the new *youth culture* of rock, dope and freaky clothes coming out of San Francisco. PL was dour and old-fashioned, a highly organized group of short-haired, well-read, thoroughly earnest kids in work clothes who might have attended union rallies in the 1930s, and were led by men who had. PL had been founded (first as the Progressive Labor Movement, later as a party) early in the 1960s by former members of the American Communist Party who sided with the militant world-revolution-now line of Peking, instead of the cautious, accommodating, "revisionist" line of Moscow. PL members were under *discipline*, which meant that decisions came down from above, rather than up from below (which was the theory, at any rate, of SDS). It also meant that they behaved as a solid bloc within SDS, forcing the New Left faction to react as a bloc in order to win crucial votes.

The struggle between PL and the New Left faction of SDS had begun quietly in January, 1966, when the May 2nd Movement (M2M), a student organization secretly controlled by PL, decided to dissolve itself and work within SDS. The national officers of SDS claimed, and probably believed, that PL was trying to take over SDS for its own purposes. According to the New Left, PL hoped to use SDS as a ready-made mass organization which could carry out PL strategy, and as a recruiting ground for future PL party members. PL denied these charges, insisting its differences with the national officers of SDS were solely ideological. The result was an atmosphere of suspicion and intrigue which had begun to polarize SDS by the time Diana and Bill arrived in East Lansing for the convention. The contest was an important one, since whoever controlled the votes at the national conventions and the (more or less) quarterly national councils would control SDS at a time when it was indisputably the one organization most respected by the rapidly expanding student movement.

Between PL and the New Left at SDS conventions there was traditionally a broad mass of unorganized student activists ranging (in 1968) from supporters of Bobby Kennedy and Eugene McCarthy to super-militant revolutionary desperadoes who argued that the moment to pick up the gun was *now*. Many of the latter were suspected (in some cases correctly) of being undercover agents.

A special workshop in sabotage and explosives was organized at the 1968 convention to draw off police spies so the other groups could carry on discussions without having to worry about being overheard in Washington. (Not all of those attending the workshop were undercover men, however. One who was, an agent from the sheriff's office in Jefferson Parish, Louisiana,* who later testified before a Senate investigating committee, said that Cathy Wilkerson had attended the sabotage workshop.)

At the end of the convention elections were held for the eight-man National Interim Committee (NIC), which made decisions between national SDS meetings, and for the three national officers. The latter included two New Left people, Mike Klonsky of California and Bernardine Dohrn of Chicago, and a neutral, Fred Gordon, vaguely suspected of being a secret PL member.

Among the new NIC members was Eric Mann, a Cornell University graduate (where he had been president of the inter-fraternity council) and a veteran of the Newark Community Union Project. Mann, too, had lived in the Felch Street commune from time to time with Bill and Diana. As members of Voice-SDS in Ann Arbor, the first and still one of the largest SDS chapters, and as friends of Mann, Chester and several other nationally known SDS members, Bill and Diana were close to the center of the six days of incessant politicking in East Lansing. Bill's unrestrained enthusiasm and high-spirited

* Police in Jefferson Parish, Louisiana, were not the only ones to take an interest in SDS conventions. Departments in Chicago, New York and elsewhere also made a practice of penetrating radical organizations. The FBI, of course, did the same.

daring quickly earned him a reputation in the organization. When two state legislators held a news conference to criticize MSU's decision to house the SDS convention, Bill clowned around with the television crews and made fun of the legislators, who were speaking in an outraged tone about hardworking taxpayers and young subversives trying to destroy Everything That Made This Country Great. From that week on, SDS and its sharpening break with American society were to dominate Diana's life.

That summer she and Bill worked in the SDS national office at 1608 West Madison Street in Chicago, where they got to know Klonsky and Bernardine Dohrn. Behind all of their discussions about day-to-day political organizing was the example of Columbia University, where American students had sparked a major crisis by abandoning argument and taking over a building. The confrontation at Columbia seemed to confirm the potential of a thesis argued by Regis Debray, the French revolutionary writer who suggested in a long essay called "Revolution in the Revolution" that elite groups could spark revolution in backward countries by taking up arms and forcing the population to choose sides. Debray's strategy had failed in Bolivia, where Che Guevara had been killed in October, 1967, and where Debray himself was serving a thirty-year jail sentence,* but it seemed to have worked at Columbia.

In spite of that success Mark Rudd, probably expecting a hero's welcome in East Lansing, had been rejected by the anti-heroic SDS convention. Nevertheless, he remained a

* Debray was freed by the Bolivian government on December 23, 1970.

national figure and the chief spokesman of a growing faction within the national organization which wanted to unite revolutionary theory with revolutionary *practice.* When realists argued that the working class was simply not ready to choose revolution in a contest between the American right and left, the "action faction" (a term introduced by Columbia SDS) countered that the young formed a class of their own with a revolutionary potential. Diana and Bill felt a sense of kinship with the apolitical young who smoked dope, listened to acid rock, lived in communes and hated the establishment, who lived in a revolutionary style even if they did not think of themselves as political revolutionaries in the traditional sense.

The events of convention week in Chicago seemed to prove the theory. Bill, Diana, and Skip Taube were among the several thousand young people who slept in the parks, marched in the streets and were attacked by the Chicago police. Diana had lunch with her sister Carol one day during the convention, used Carol's hotel room on another occasion and finally borrowed $150 from her to help bail Tom Hayden out of jail after he had been arrested. The week of violence permanently changed the political attitudes of Bill and Diana. Bill carried a white, water-soaked cloth as protection against tear gas and, with his usual enthusiasm, pointed out to a friend how he had chosen clothes which would make it hard for the police to grab him. Nevertheless, one succeeded and Bill was severely clubbed. Diana called her sister to say she and Bill were leaving Chicago. "It's getting too rough," she said.

When Bill returned to Ann Arbor, his head was swathed in bandages, but he was elated by the fact that demonstrators had stayed in the streets. They had not fought back, but they had refused to surrender their rights of protest. The result had been a moral victory, a vivid revelation of the police brutality by which the establishment maintained itself, and stillbirth for Hubert Humphrey's presidential campaign.

Chicago seemed to prove that persuasion was not going to change America. McCarthy and his movement had obeyed all the rules and had been clubbed and teargassed for their efforts. All year SDS had felt its support slipping as thousands of students were swept up by the excitement of the McCarthy and Kennedy campaigns. The assassination of Kennedy and the strong-armed defeat of McCarthy left SDS, in the minds of thousands of young people, as one of the few alternatives to the America of Chicago's Mayor Richard Daley. Chicago seemed to prove that America was on the verge of breaking down. Going into the streets, Bill felt, had ripped the liberal mask from Daley's face and left him, plainly visible to millions over television, shouting his scorn at the young, the poor, and the black. Daley's police won the battle but lost the war. Klonsky told a reporter from the Cuban revolutionary newspaper *Granma* that Chicago had been a political victory for SDS and the American student movement. "We managed to outsmart, outfight and outmaneuver them," he said.

In August and early September Ayers joined a Cleveland, Ohio, SDS organizer named Terry Robbins on a tour of Midwestern campuses. They helped local SDS chapters stage demonstrations and recruit members in the first of a series of attempts to prove the potential of what they had been arguing in theory: young people were ready to revolt. At Kent State University they prodded the local SDS chapter, formed the previous February, into sponsoring a guerrilla-theater performance and a heavily attended acid rock concert. At the chapter's first organizational meeting more than sixty students showed up, a sizable turnout.

At Case Western Reserve University in Cleveland, Ayers and Robbins handed out SDS leaflets during freshman orientation week and then held a shouting, chanting, fist-shaking demonstration in front of a downtown hotel where Humphrey was spending the night. The result was another Humphrey campaign story dominated by student heckling. In a report on their efforts published in the October 7 issue of the SDS newspaper, *New Left Notes,* Ayers and Robbins described the message they were bringing to disillusioned students, bitter about McCarthy's defeat in Chicago, sick of the endless war in Vietnam, angry at the society which had allowed both:

> We're saying to people that youth is the revolution, that politics is about life, struggle, survival. We're saying there ain't no place to be today but in the movement. And we're saying to kids all over the place that if you're tired of the Vietnamese eating napalm for breakfast, if you're tired of the blacks eating tear gas for dinner, and if *you're* tired of eating plastic for lunch, then give it a name: Call it SDS, and join us.

Back in Ann Arbor, Ayers, Terry Robbins and another stranger to the University of Michigan, Jim Mellen, made plans to capture control of the sober and intellectual SDS chapter at the university. Centering on the Felch Street commune, the group at first called itself the Lurleen Wallace Memorial Caucus (after the late wife of former Alabama Governor George Wallace, then running a third-party campaign for the presidency) but finally settled on another name which captured a hint of the new mood they intended to inject into SDS: the Jesse James Gang.

At the first meeting of Voice-SDS on Tuesday, September 25, 1968, the James Gang launched a whistling, shouting, foot-stamping assault on the old leadership. They charged the group with being reformist and timid, "a polite inoffensive fart in the drawing room of the university." The old leadership denounced the attack as heckling but Ayers insisted they were only trying to "open up the discussion." The Gang ridiculed previous SDS campaigns, principally a year-long organizing attempt to discredit war research carried on at the University of Michigan under the aegis of the Institute for Defense Analysis (IDA). The campaign, characterized by a button with the legend GO MICHIGAN — BEAT THAILAND, had involved speeches, petitions and leafleting. Eventually the university's Student Government Council took up the issue and sponsored a university-wide referendum on war research and affiliation with the IDA. The result: a heavy turnout by the School of Engineering and decisive rejection of the SDS proposals. Where did that leave SDS? Ayers wanted to know. Was war research all right, now that it had received democratic approval?

"We are tired of tiptoeing up to society and asking for reform," Ayers said at one point. "We're ready to kick it in the balls."

The majority of SDS, however, was not. During the following weeks the Jesse James Gang and their opponents, who organized themselves as the Radical Caucus, struggled in long meetings over action versus broad-based organizing. The Radical Caucus insisted that premature action would simply alienate the vast majority of American society. The Gang insisted that action was the only thing likely to create a situation in which radical solutions to American problems would be considered. "The argument is not between radical action and building a mass movement," Ayers said at one meeting, "but whether education can *ever* build a mass movement."

At its simplest, the argument could be reduced to a difference of opinion about the extent of support radicals enjoyed throughout the student community. The James Gang was arguing that, in fact, radicals had a large, submerged following. The way to prove the point, they said in effect, was to give society a punch in the nose and then look around to see who applauded.

When Robben Fleming, president of the university, gave a speech in late September the James Gang staged a demonstration outside the building. Her short hair held back by a headband, Diana spoke to the group, using a public-address system, while other Gang members handed out slices of bread and shouted, "Here's the bread, get the baloney inside." Inside, Gang members disrupted Fleming's speech from the back of the room, shouting "What about the war?" It was exactly the sort of thing the old Voice-SDS would never have done.

The conflict between the James Gang and the Radical Caucus steadily sharpened. Gang members let selected opponents know they might be facing physical beatings if they kept on as they had, while Radical Caucus members denounced Terry Robbins as an outsider and suggested that Jim Mellen, over thirty, might even be an *agent provocateur* sent in by the CIA.

Little was known of Mellen, who told people only that he had spent the last few years in Tanzania. He had arrived in Ann Arbor in September, seemingly out of nowhere, confident, articulate, even ingratiating when he showed up at the office of the Michigan *Daily* to establish relations with the local reporters and editors. He seemed to know exactly what he was about. Even those who doubted that Mellen was working for the CIA were not altogether sure whom he *was* working for, since at one time he had been closely connected with the Progressive Labor Party in New York. As secretary treasurer of the Free University in the fall of 1965, Mellen was in frequent contact with Milt Rosen, the chairman of PL, and Russell Stetler, a founder of M2M, both of whom taught at the Free University. Mellen had also been connected with M2M outside the Free University, but it was not known if he had been one of the secret PL members who effectively controlled the organization. The most likely explanation was that Mellen was simply another of those unaffiliated, full-time revolutionaries who had always existed in American society.

Like the others, many of whom were PL members in the early 1960s, Mellen gravitated to organizations with a broad appeal, and in the fall of 1968 by far the largest and most vital of such groups was the SDS. Whatever the doubts about Mellen's precise background, there was no questioning his formidable political talents. One of the Radical Caucus's criticisms of Ayers was his almost total unfamiliarity with the literature of revolution. Mellen, a persuasive speaker and relentless polemicist, was also thoroughly acquainted with Hegel, Marx, Engels, Lenin, Mao and dozens of other revolutionary writers. When arguments degenerated into quoting the sacred texts of the left, Mellen was likely to come out ahead.

The James Gang never managed to muster the votes necessary to control Voice-SDS, but they continually harassed the Radical Caucus, which was anxious to get on with its own plans. The fourth meeting of the fall was scheduled for Tuesday, October 15. On the fourteenth the Radical Caucus met and voted to leave SDS in order to start its own chapter, since the SDS constitution provided that any five people could declare themselves an SDS chapter. In less than a month the James Gang had captured the University of Michigan chapter of SDS, although not until they had driven away more than half the chapter's membership. Nevertheless, this put Ayers, Robbins and Mellen in a strong position to control SDS throughout the state and, with allies in Ohio and Illinois, throughout the entire Midwest. With the Midwest as a base, the national organization was within range.

In an article in the *New Left Notes* of November 11, Ayers, Robbins and Mellen, writing jointly, described the Ann Arbor takeover and the reasoning behind it. The old argument that building a base had to precede mass action had been disproved by the events of 1968, they argued.

> Things were happening. Radical politics wasn't turning *everybody* off. Somebody was in those buildings. Somebody was in the streets of Chicago.

> We began to feel, for the first time, that the situation was real. Not tomorrow. Or the next year. But real. We began to feel that our movement had something to offer to people: not just a rejection of plastic, cool-slick computerized America, but positive things: the way they lived in the buildings at Columbia, the way we developed community in Chicago's only more overt police state. A new culture, liberated, vibrant, audacious. A new style of activism — saying and doing who you really are. And now belief in yourself as a person really able to understand freedom, and to fight for it.

The activist faction within SDS was also in control when the fall National Council (NC) was held at the University of Colorado in Boulder between October 10 and 12. Diana was a member of the group from Ann Arbor. Ideological bickering was at a minimum, since PL was so badly outnumbered that their only serious proposal was defeated 80 to 40. (PL later charged the National Office with stacking the meeting by crediting 20 phony delegates. They quoted Klonsky as saying after the lop-

sided vote, "It was stupid for those people to vote because we didn't need them.") In return for permission to
meet on university property the SDS had agreed to
allow newsmen to attend their sessions, but they balked
at the presence of microphones and cameras. An ugly
incident occurred when a CBS cameraman was roughed
up after he insisted on bringing his equipment into the
meeting room.

Plans for organizing an election protest were over-
shadowed by a new sense of excitement and solidarity
which bound the New Left people together. Klonsky later
said the Boulder NC was the beginning of the "national
collective," a like-minded group which included the New
Left faction in the national office, allies in Chicago SDS,
and organizers from all over the country who happened to
be passing through. The council also reorganized SDS
into regional areas which would carry activity beyond
the confines of college campuses. The new sense of militance carried over into Sunday, when a number of New
Left delegates, including Diana, remained to discuss the
newly developing notion of youth culture as all those
things which alienated young people regardless of their
class origins.

Leading the discussion was the SDS chapter from New
York's Lower East Side known as the "Motherfuckers."
The first of the new communal street-fighting affinity
groups, the group had been given chapter status at the
Lexington, Kentucky, NC held March 28–31, 1968. (Its
name came from a line in a poem by LeRoi Jones, "Up
against the wall, Motherfucker." Mark Rudd had used the

line to end a letter to Columbia University President Grayson Kirk and it became a slogan during the uprising, a gesture of defiance which stood for a hard-line refusal to compromise by students who insisted, for the first time, that the free society had to come before the free university.) At Boulder the Motherfuckers argued that militant political action could capture the allegiance of thousands of young dropouts living in hippie and working-class communities who would be turned off by the "intellectual bullshit" of traditional radicals.

On their way back from the Boulder NC Diana and Kathy Boudin, who had graduated from Bryn Mawr two years after Diana, stopped off in Chicago and had dinner with Diana's old college friend, Karin Carlson Rosenberg. Diana was still excited by the four-day meeting in Boulder, certain that a genuine revolutionary ferment was rising in America, that SDS was at its center and that Bill and she were part of the cutting edge within SDS. Karin's husband, Merrill, taught classes in French literature at the University of Chicago and was a lover of good food and wine. He and his wife lived off Lake Shore Drive in a comfortable apartment filled with books and furnished in simple modern furniture; but Diana and Kathy found it the height of middle-class bourgeois pretension. "The only people I know who live like this," said Kathy, "are friends of my parents."

Most of the evening's conversation centered on the conflict between their life styles: Diana and Kathy totally committed to the revolution, Karin and Merrill appreciating the good things of life and relaxed about political questions. When the subject of women's liberation came up, Diana mentioned her anger at the film *Barbarella* for treating Jane Fonda as a sexual object in a demeaning way. They also talked about drugs, Kathy expressing a prudish dislike for any kind of tampering with the mind. Diana said she and Bill had taken LSD a couple of times the previous summer, including one occasion with another couple when one of the group had run out into the street naked. The rest of the group managed to coax him back in before the police arrived, she said.

Most of the conversation centered on politics, ending with a long argument between Diana and Merrill. Diana would list all the things SDS wanted to change in American society with Merrill agreeing, as often as not, that this or that seemed like an outrage to him, too. "How can you think that way and then do nothing?" Diana demanded.

"That's just not the sort of person I am," Merrill said.

Diana insisted that revolution was the only way to solve America's problems and that she was a revolutionary. Merrill, knowing he was being challenged, doubted that marching and picketing really qualified as revolutionary activity. Revolution meant violence. "If you're really serious you're going to have to throw bombs," he said, strongly implying that he felt Diana would back down long before reaching that point. "That's the way to get the widest reply."

Back at Ann Arbor Diana helped organize demonstrations against the "election fraud." Michigan Secretary of State James Hare called a news conference to charge

that SDS was planning to use bombs and Molotov cock-
tails to disrupt polling places, but the SDS actions were
all peaceful. On Monday, November 4, SDS conducted a
tour of the University of Michigan emphasizing "coun-
ter-insurgency institutions" like the school of international affairs and ROTC. That night a torchlight parade
grew to more than 2000 by the time it reached Robben
Fleming's residence. On Tuesday SDS sponsored a four-
hour occupation of Fleming's office. Thousands of students heard SDS speakers ridicule the Humphrey-Nixon,
Tweedledum-Tweedledee choice and were inclined to
agree that the election was, in fact, a kind of fraud.

Weatherman

DIANA'S SENSE OF herself as a revolutionary made it steadily more difficult to get along with her family. On trips home arguments with her father contained a note of bitterness. Dwight was a complacent backwater; her parents knew only indirectly of the passions sweeping college campuses, of the anger beginning to color the thinking of students. America seemed serene and secure from Dwight; in the ghettos of Chicago and Detroit the country seemed ready to explode. Diana's father argued from a perspective forged during three decades. He had come home from Dartmouth College in 1935. He had seen the depression and World War II test the stability of America, and had seen America survive and grow. Diana knew only the desperation of a generation that felt it was being pressed into an immoral, unconstitutional war in Vietnam. Diana knew that dreams of vengeance burned in the hearts of America's children; her father knew the society would survive.

Mr. Oughton enjoyed argument and pressed his daughter on political questions. Their views were so far apart, however, that political discussions inevitably veered toward acrimony. When Diana and her father began to argue, Mrs. Oughton, uninterested in politics, would often retreat to her room. Mr. Oughton would ask what SDS planned to create in the place of American society as it was. Diana would argue that anything would be an improvement. Mr. Oughton would ask what she found so admirable about the totalitarian regimes of Russia, China and Cuba. Diana would dismiss the question as red-baiting, while pointing out that the United States could be repressive, too.

In essence their differences reduced to a fundamental conflict of moral vision. Mr. Oughton conceded that a lot of things were wrong with America, but argued that the democratic process, as slow and erratic as it was, still remained the best means of reform. Diana felt that American racism at home and American imperialism in Vietnam were intolerable crimes, that a complacent willingness to live with those crimes while American democracy stumbled toward their solution amounted to criminal complicity. Mr. Oughton could live with America as it was; Diana could not. Argument could never reconcile their differences. "I've made my decision, Daddy," she said on one of her infrequent visits to Dwight. "There's no sense talking about it."

In some ways Mr. Oughton found it easier to talk politics with Bill Ayers or the other Ann Arbor friends Diana often brought home with her, most of whom Mr. Oughton considered witless and dull. Their conversation often seemed a giggling, smirking, self-congratulatory stew of phrases like "Oh, wow," "Far out," "Outtasight" and "Get it together." They were confident to the point of arrogance. Once Diana's mother asked in her tentative, almost pained way what some of Diana's friends believed in. Their answer was open ridicule; she never asked again.

Mr. Oughton was once astonished to see them react in a similar fashion to a similar question from the youth who mowed the Oughtons' lawn. On other occasions, however, the conversations he had with Diana's friends were positively chilling. Diana once stopped by with some friends on their way to a teach-in. One of the group was a middle-aged, bearded professor who freely conceded that democracy was obsolete because most of the people were not qualified to decide what was good for them. "The majority is never right," the professor said. "We'll just have to line them up against the wall and shoot them."

Mr. Oughton was naturally disturbed to find his daughter at ease with tough-talking kids who struck him as nothing more than window-breaking vandals, as well as with hardened ideologues who betrayed a grim pleasure in talking about what would happen to their enemies after the revolution. Diana felt that political arguments with her father were getting nowhere, but he couldn't leave the subject alone. Sometimes she used to kid him when his questions betrayed a lack of familiarity with American radical politics. Once he asked seriously where SDS was getting its instructions and money.

"Peking, Daddy," she answered.

That fall Diana also lost contact with a number of old friends. She wrote Mike Kimmell in November, vague about her plans but including a quote from D. H. Lawrence which she said expressed what she had been trying to say about social commitment while sitting next to Kimmell on the plane to Guatemala five years earlier. "There is no point in work unless it absorbs you like an interesting game," she quoted Lawrence. "If it doesn't absorb you, if it's not any fun, don't do it."

Kimmell's first reaction was ungenerous: "With her money, she can afford to think that way."

Later, he decided he had been wrong. Remembering the way Diana had worked in Guatemala, Kimmell felt she had not been telling the truth about herself, that embarrassment made her try to disguise her almost puritanical seriousness and devotion to hard work; that, in fact, Diana always did what she thought was her duty, whether she liked it or not. Kimmell never heard from her again.

During the same period Diana also stopped seeing Doris Cummings. That summer Doris invited Diana to attend a church service where Doris was going to be singing a solo. To her surprise, Diana came. After the service Diana said the minister had irritated her. "I felt everything he was saying was pointed directly at me," she said. Walking home, Diana asked Doris how she could put up with the racism that went along with fundamentalist Christianity in America. Doris tried to explain what the Gospel message meant to her. "Well," Diana said quietly, "if it works for you then that's all right."

She saw Doris again, briefly, in September, but never again, despite the fact she lived in Ann Arbor for most of the next year and passed through periodically after that until the time of her death. After leaving Bryn Mawr, Diana saw little of her Bryn Mawr friends. After leaving Guatemala, she saw little of people she had known there. After leaving the Children's Community School, she stopped seeing most of the children and parents. Each stage of her life was cut off from the preceding stage.

On December 9 Diana wrote home trying to define the things which separated her from her family:

> It gets harder, and I get more reluctant to justify myself over and over again to you. It's a very defensive position to continually be put in. I feel as if I've gone through a process of conscious choice, and that I've thought about it a lot and that people I admire agree with me. Educationally important and recognized and respected people respect us. I feel like a moral person, that my life is my values, that most people my age or even younger have already begun to sell out to materialism, status, hypocrisy, stepping on other people, etc. Politically, I'm not surprised you don't understand. I feel like part of a vanguard, that we speak of important change to come . . . It doesn't seem unreasonable to me that I would want you to accept me as I am, to meet my friends and accept my relationship with Bill. I don't want to hide things from you or pussyfoot around, especially since I'm not ashamed of my life, but am proud of it.

During the fall the SDS national office in Chicago made Diana a regional organizer for Michigan, at least partly to forestall criticism by the women's liberation movement that SDS was male chauvinist. Like most of the other women in SDS Diana considered women's liberation important only insofar as it gave women the right to be the revolutionary equals of men. Issues like abortion-law reform and discrimination in hiring did not much interest her. At a time when most women in the movement were touchy to the point of hysteria about their dignity, Diana was relaxed and realistic, one of the few SDS females who could be called a girl without starting a fight. All the others insisted they were *women;* Diana never insisted, but was automatically considered one.

After the Jesse James Gang took over SDS in Ann Arbor (ending its faint ties to the memory of Voice), the national office decided to hold the December NC at the University of Michigan. The Midwest was becoming a national collective stronghold while PL was largely confined to the East and West Coasts. Nevertheless, when the council convened its first plenary session in the giant cafeteria in the university's dormitory complex the day after Christmas, 1968, it was clear that PL had arrived in strength. Throughout the five-day conference, ending New Year's Eve, the voting balanced delicately between the national collective and PL. There were three crucial resolutions at the convention, concerning the so-called *national question;* Mike Klonsky's proposal for turning SDS into a Revolutionary Youth Movement; and a dispute between Klonsky-Dohrn and Fred Gordon over the printing of a

pamphlet. The national collective won on the first two issues, which continued to dominate SDS internal politics
for the following six months, and managed to obtain a
compromise on the last.

Put simply, the national question involved the correct
analysis of the position of blacks in America: were they a
separate people who formed a colony within the United
States (as the national collective and the Black Panthers
claimed), or were they simply super-exploited members of
the working class facing the added problem of racial discrimination (as PL maintained)? Behind the question of
definition was a far more important point, often hidden to
those unfamiliar with PL–New Left infighting: the national collective and the Panthers insisted the Panthers
were the *vanguard of the revolution* (in revolutionary
terms, the immediate source of the revolution), while PL
insisted that *it* was the vanguard.

The significance of this dispute was practical and immediate: the central committee of PL insisted that it
should be directing all revolutionary activity in the United
States, while the central committee of the Panthers felt
that honor belonged to them. In fact, of course, the national collective, although siding with the Panthers, did
not really intend to let the Panthers run the revolution,
but instead hoped that the popular charisma of the Panthers (who had the virtue of being both black and Marxist-Leninist) would sway the uncommitted middle at the
December NC. As it turned out, they were right. Despite
the collective's victory in Ann Arbor, its arguments were
far less coherent, and less solidly grounded in Marxist-

Leninist theory, than the positions argued by PL. Typically, the Panthers were not present at the NC even though they provided one of the chief subjects of discussion.

The fight over Klonsky's proposal to begin building a *youth* movement hinged on a number of similar arguments. The national collective argued that young people could be considered as a class by themselves, at least for the purposes of organizing, since college kids and working-class kids all liked rock music, smoked dope and were harassed by the police. PL, which rigorously suppressed anything that might offend the highly conservative American working class, insisted, again, that young people might have their special problems but were still only a subgroup within the working class. Klonsky summed up the dispute in an interview with a reporter from the about-to-be-launched Ann Arbor *Argus*:

> PL's analysis is sectarian, see, because it doesn't understand the need for people to fight as a nation or a black people, or as women, or as youth for liberation apart from the class struggle.

Again, the real issue was who was going to run the revolution.

The conflicts buried in these two disputes emerged as an overt power struggle in the argument over the pamphlet which Klonsky-Dohrn had refused to print at SDS expense. The pamphlet reported on the PL–Worker Student Alliance (PL-WSA) summer project of 1968. Klonsky-Dohrn had refused to print it because they didn't like its politics. The national collective finally agreed to print 15,000 copies of the pamphlet so long as it contained a disclaimer saying, "These are the political views of one tendency within SDS."

The council also decided not to co-sponsor a Washington demonstration at the inauguration of President-elect Richard Nixon in spite of the national collective's support for the proposal. It was decided there was not enough time to adequately prepare for the action, less than three weeks away, but a number of SDS chapters took part anyway.

Diana's only public role in the December NC came on Sunday night, December 29, during a credentials fight. The Radical Caucus which had walked out of Ann Arbor SDS in October now applied for chapter status but was turned down after Diana, among others, argued that granting the request would only tend to fragment the movement. If Radical Caucus members wanted to rejoin Ann Arbor SDS individually, she said, they would be welcome to do so.

When the council ended on New Year's Eve the national officers made the traditional appeal for funds. In the past the fund-raising had always been accompanied by the singing of revolutionary songs, but this time the room was divided into chanting factions trying to drown each other with cries of "Ho Ho Ho Chi Minh" (by national collective people) and "Mao Mao Mao Tse-tung" (by PL people, who considered Ho a sellout for negotiating with the United States in Paris).

The infighting at the council had been more vicious

The townhouse at 18 West Eleventh Street was completely destroyed by the bomb that exploded on March 6, 1970, and the fire that followed it. Diana Oughton was standing next to a workbench in the basement when the bomb exploded a foot or two away from her. *Below:* Firemen remove the remains of Diana Oughton's body from the wrecked house on March 10, four days after the explosion killed her and two other Weathermen. It took the police another week to identify her. *(United Press International Photos)*

In the fall of 1956, Diana left Dwight for the Madeira School in Greenway, Virginia. This photograph was taken during her years at high school. (*United Press International Photo*)

The Oughton house in Dwight, Illinois. (*United Press International Photo*)

The grounds of the original Oughton estate.
(Hedrich Blessing)

In 1964, Diana worked with the poverty-stricken Indians in the market town of Chichicastenango, Guatemala. She was especially fond of the Indian children. *Below:* Diana with her childhood nurse, Ruth Morehart, sitting in the Oughtons' living room in Dwight.

(United Press International Photos)

In 1966, Diana Oughton joined the Children's Community School in Ann Arbor, Michigan, where she met Bill Ayers. Here she is shown with one of the children in 1967. The school was closed in 1968 for lack of funds. (*United Press International Photo*)

On a rare trip home in 1967, Diana surprised her family by agreeing to attend a cousin's debutante party. Dressed in formal clothes for perhaps the last time, Diana drinks a toast with her father.
(United Press International Photo)

Alan Howard met Diana when she was working in Guatemala. A graduate of Hamilton College and a Fulbright scholar, he told her that her work was "only delaying the revolution." *Below:* Bill Ayers, one of the three national officers elected by the Weatherman faction of SDS, was Diana's boy friend. Their close relationship drew Diana increasingly deeper into radical circles. *(United Press International Photos)*

Bill Ayers (center in shorts and checked shirt) joins in the singing of the "Internationale" at the 1968 national convention of SDS held at Michigan State University in East Lansing. *(Thomas R. Copi)*

Left: Diana Oughton addresses a rally on the steps of the Rackham Building on the University of Michigan campus in October of 1968. *(Thomas R. Copi)*

Bernadine Dohrn, shown here addressing a rally in Chicago in September of 1969, became a rival to Diana for Bill Ayers's attentions. *(United Press International Photo)*

Chicago plainclothes police subdue one of a dozen Weatherwomen who charged into police lines in Grant Park on October 9, 1969. Diana Oughton was at the demonstration. *(United Press International Photo)*

Weathermen attack a Chicago policeman during the last of the Four Days of Rage, October 11, 1969. The arrow points to the policeman's visor, knocked flying in the attack. *(United Press International Photo)*

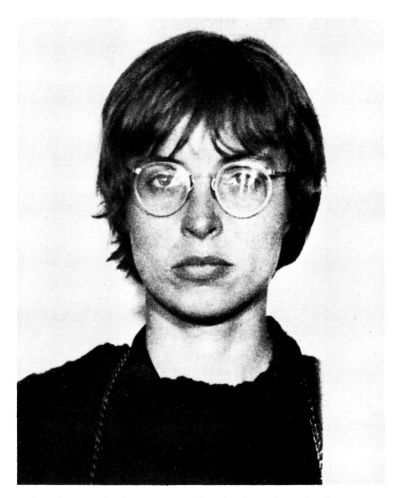

This photograph of Diana was taken by the police after her arrest for participation in the all-women action held in Chicago's Grant Park in October, 1969. The fingerprints taken at the same time were eventually used to identify her body in March, 1970. *(United Press International Photo)*

and determined than usual. Fred Gordon charged that he had been physically threatened during a meeting of the national officers with the NIC in a basement room. The national collective said Gordon was paranoid. Gordon countered that the national collective had planned the whole thing so he would *seem* to be paranoid. During one caucus of the Jesse James Gang Jim Mellen successfully urged the Gang to throw out people suspected of being spies for the Radical Caucus. The Gang also spread the word that their opponents were again running the risk of a beating.

Following the conference Daniel Okrent, editor of the Michigan *Daily* and a friend of Bill Ayers, attacked the James Gang in a long article for practicing a variety of fascism. Okrent's attitude toward the increasingly high-handed James Gang was widely shared. The Gang's control of SDS in Ann Arbor was unchallenged by the beginning of 1969, but the chapter also had less support on the University of Michigan campus than at any other time since the founding of SDS six years earlier.

Despite the attack Ayers continued to drop by the *Daily* occasionally for a few hands in the nightly poker game, Diana often sitting quietly to one side while Bill played. It was clear, however, that radical politics was developing a poisonous side, upsetting to many who had known SDS in the old days. When individuals slipped out of phase with some of the Gang's ideas, they were given a stark choice: get in line or get out. The situation was the same at Columbia and elsewhere. SDS felt its opposition to American society was *total*: people temperamentally inclined to argue on the one hand this, on the other hand that were no longer welcome. There were *right* political opinions and there were *wrong* ones; people with the *wrong* opinions were not to be tolerated.

Throughout the winter and early spring of 1969 Diana, Bill, Jim Mellen, Terry Robbins and other members of the James Gang tried out their theories of confrontation at several Midwestern universities, but not, for a variety of reasons, at the University of Michigan. In January and February they all drove to East Lansing to take part in a struggle over Michigan State University's refusal to grant tenure to a popular psychology professor, Bert Garskoff, a radical who gave automatic A's to all of his students.

The SDS in East Lansing had been enervated all year by an unresolved struggle between its New Left and PL factions. At a planning meeting held Wednesday night, January 29, 1969, Ayers took the side of the new left and proposed an immediate building takeover, arguing that the issue was right, the students were angry and the time had come to *move*. The PL-WSA people defeated his motion. Rallies and meetings accomplished little during the following few days and Ayers repeated his proposal at another meeting on Sunday, February 2. This time it carried. On Monday, nearly 1200 students occupied an administration building but left almost immediately after the university called in the police.

Organizing around Garskoff's tenure and open admissions (tacked on to give the conflict a political dimension) continued for another couple of weeks without accomplishing anything concrete, but Bill and Diana felt the campaign had been a success anyway. The students had taken militant action to correct what they saw as an injustice. The university's reliance on the police defeated the students' immediate aims but seemed to confirm SDS's contention that the establishment maintained itself only through violence. The failure to win their demands convinced students the struggle had to be widened. Since they were right, the system either had to give in or be overthrown. Diana and Bill felt the conflict had increased the revolutionary consciousness of a significant number of MSU students.

During one of the actions at MSU Bill got into a dispute with a cameraman from a Detroit television station. He smashed the man's camera and early in February was arrested on a charge of assault, despite the fact he had not actually touched the cameraman himself. (One of Diana's dividend checks went toward his bail.) Bill considered his arrest part of an attack on SDS by the state.

Earlier that winter the state legislature had announced it would investigate SDS. When the Radical Education Project (REP) office in Ann Arbor was burglarized on the night of February 7, the SDS, which shared REP's office, darkly implied that state officials were responsible. The only things taken, SDS pointed out, were financial records, mailing lists, correspondence and the names of SDS contacts at schools throughout Michigan. Glass cutters had been used and the fuse box had been emptied, hardly the signs of amateurs. Bill and Diana felt repression was finally beginning.

The burglary was not the only instance of harassment suffered by SDS. Their phone was often disconnected or simply out of order and whenever SDS tried to rent office space they ran into difficulty.

At the end of March, Ayers and Mellen went to the SDS National Council held in a Catholic student center near the University of Texas campus, where they had been refused permission to meet. PL was badly outnumbered at the Austin council and a resolution by Ayers and Mellen for a militant summer-organizing program was easily passed. The proposal, titled "Hot Town — Summer in the City," called for a variation on the PL-WSA work-in, emphasizing the building of alliances with working-class youth around issues of youth culture rather than wages and other traditional working-class issues.

Gradually Michigan-Ohio SDS, along with SDS at Columbia in New York, was emerging as an action-oriented bloc within SDS. The momentum was maintained that spring with a series of militant (but unsuccessful) actions at Kent State University. On Tuesday, April 8, 1969, about 200 students led by SDS marched through classrooms following a rally protesting university disciplinary proceedings and just over a week later, on Wednesday, April 16, Jim Mellen addressed another, much larger rally:

> I know there are some pigs out there who still think we should occupy Vietnam. And there are some pigs out there who still think they can go into the ghettos and push people around. Well, what we're telling you is that you can't do it anymore! We are no longer asking you to come

and help us make a revolution. We're telling you that the revolution has begun, and the only choice you have to make is which side you're on. And we're also telling you that if you get in the way of the revolution, it's going to run right over you!

After the rally about 700 people marched to the building where a disciplinary hearing was being held, fought with some anti-SDS athletes outside and forced an entrance for about 150 demonstrators. Police closed in quickly, however, and 58 students were arrested. Again, the spirits of SDS were high despite the failure of an action nominally intended to win a concrete objective.

In New York City, much the same thing was happening at Columbia University, where the SDS initiated actions again and again without being able to seriously disrupt the university. On the second day of the April, 1968, uprising thousands of students had stood in a pouring rain outside the occupied buildings, debating with themselves whether or not to join those inside, and with each other about the issues behind the occupations. During the spring of 1969 the SDS attracted little attention at Columbia despite its willingness to engage in far more daring actions. The failure of the strategy of exemplary action did not convince them the strategy was fundamentally wrong, however. At Columbia and in the Middle West elite actions failed to win wide support but nevertheless resulted in a cadre of committed friends who became what newsmen always liked to call a *hard core*. They were like the skeleton of an army, officers and sergeants who lacked only troops.

During the first half of 1969 SDS was engaged in what amounted to a prolonged experiment: they were trying to find a way in which revolutionaries could *create* a revolutionary situation, rather than submitting to the exigencies of history and waiting for such a situation to create itself. SDS felt that generations of American radicals had wasted their lives and strength waiting for the right moment to arrive; SDS wanted to seize the moment, to bring the flow of history under its control, to spark the explosion which would tear open the American imperial monster. Their own failures seemed less important than the successes of others. During the spring of 1969 it sometimes seemed that the explosions of discontent which disrupted one university after another might suddenly jell into a single nationwide upheaval. Early in the year the National Guard was called out during student actions at Berkeley, at the University of Wisconsin and at Duke. In April, black students with guns cowed the administration of Cornell University. That same month the SDS (controlled, ironically, by PL) precipitated a crisis at Harvard University. In May black students shut down City College in New York while a new crisis at Berkeley erupted over the People's Park. The struggle was escalating: Berkeley police fired buckshot at demonstrators, killing one of them. At City College students fought each other with clubs and burned a building. The SDS had reason to believe the situation was approaching a critical point.

Convinced that determined action by a small group could force larger segments of society into motion, the

Michigan-Ohio-Columbia axis in SDS made plans to expel PL at the annual June convention. A major document offering an alternative to PL's tradition-bound analysis of the world situation was written for the convention, large parts of it by Jim Mellen in Ann Arbor and John Jacobs at Columbia. The document was published in the June 18 issue of *New Left Notes* under a title borrowed from Bob Dylan's song, "Subterranean Homesick Blues": "You don't need a weatherman to know which way the wind blows." The document provided a detailed alternative to PL's view of the world situation, and then proposed the creation of a revolutionary organization which would eventually be in a position to take power in the United States.

The "Weatherman" argument was that the world revolution was already under way in Vietnam and other parts of Asia, Africa and Latin America. As predicted by the Communist Chinese General Lin Piao in a 1965 paper called "Long Live the Peoples' War," the "countryside" of the world was going to rise up and swallow the "cities." American radicals, the SDS said, should forget local issues in the United States, develop an internationalist attitude, and side with the anti-imperialist struggle going on throughout the world. In America, the revolution was obviously coming from the blacks, who formed a dissident colony at the strategic heart of the country. The "Weatherman" document served two principal purposes: it provided a world view with which to fight PL, and it provided a theoretical basis for taking militant action immediately. At the same time it created a name for the SDS faction variously called the New Left, the national office, or the national collective. When the convention began, this faction referred to itself as the Revolutionary Youth Movement (RYM, pronounced "rim"), but after the convention it adopted the name of its manifesto and became Weatherman.

The national officers in Chicago were cautious in picking a convention site, being turned down by dozens of schools now thoroughly frightened by SDS, and themselves turning down suggestions for sites in New England, where PL was strong. They finally decided on the Chicago Coliseum, an aging, gray building on the city's South Side. Both major factions in SDS, knowing that a critical contest was approaching, encouraged sympathizers from every part of the country to converge on Chicago for what was obviously going to be a showdown.

The convention opened on Wednesday, June 18, 1969, while Chicago police in a building across the street used telephoto lenses to photograph conventioneers. When the opening session was finally called to order at 2:00 P.M., five hours late, it was clear PL was present in strength. PL and its caucus within SDS, the Worker Student Alliance (WSA), probably controlled fewer than half the votes, but the neutral middle tended toward PL's sober-sided view of revolution in America. On the first day Mike Klonsky lost a vote on whether or not to admit reporters from the establishment press. (The reporters were barred, but managed to cover the convention by working out deals with SDS members in need of money.)

For the first three days the balance of power tipped back and forth as PL and RYM maneuvered to find an issue which would provide either with a decisive advantage. The national question gradually emerged as the most important, or at least the most explosive, before the convention, and RYM decided to use the Black Panthers, opposed by PL, to swing sentiment in RYM's direction. On Friday, June 20, RYM arranged for an officer of the Illinois Black Panthers to address the convention. PL, knowing that police harassment of the Panthers had given the group charismatic appeal in movement circles, was cautious in its response when Panther Chaka Walls got up to speak. It was immediately apparent that RYM had made a serious mistake. Walls was aggressive and simplistic, pugnacious and insulting, speaking loosely about revolutionary theory he apparently did not understand. "If you can't relate to Huey P. Newton then you can close up your red book," Walls said. Almost everybody in the auditorium knew that relating to Huey P. Newton had little to do with the national question. Walls's intellectual crudeness began to outweigh the audience's natural sympathy with the Panthers. Disaster (from RYM's point of view) struck when Walls began to talk about the position of women in the revolution, a subject which was beginning to be taken *very* seriously by all women members of SDS.

Walls: "We believe in the freedom of love, in pussy power."

(*General embarrassment on the floor.*)

PL members (*tentatively at first*): "Fight male chauvinism!"

Walls: "We've got some puritans in the crowd. Superman was a punk because he never tried to fuck Lois Lane."

PL (*more aggressively*): "Fight Male Chauvinism!!!"

(*Walls abandons the microphone. About 7:00 P.M. another Panther, Jewell Cook, tries to make amends.*)

Cook: "I don't want to get personal but I bet PL ain't leading any struggles on campus. Call Chairman Mao and ask him who's the vanguard party in the U.S. He (*referring to Walls*) was only trying to say that you sisters have a strategic position for the revolution — prone."

(*General pandemonium on the floor.*)

PL (*delighted*): "FIGHT MALE CHAUVINISM!!!!!" *

At about 9:45 P.M. Mark Rudd proposed a one-hour recess so both factions could caucus and decide what to do. The motion failed to come to a vote. Rudd, Klonsky, Bernardine Dohrn and other RYM leaders conferred hurriedly at one end of the dais. A few minutes later Bernardine took the microphone and, in words no one seemed to remember later, announced that RYM was walking out. She marched from the dais and out of the room as other RYM leaders, and followers, hesitated in confusion and then filed out behind her. While RYM marched out the PL-WSA people stamped their feet, banged their chairs on the floor and chanted, "Stay and struggle," "No split," "Sit down."

On Saturday, June 21, RYM held an all-day caucus

* As quoted in Jack Smith's account of the convention in the *Guardian,* June 28, 1969.

to decide what to do. The disastrous performance of the Panthers had swung convention sentiment into the PL-WSA camp. If RYM went back SDS would pass into the hands of PL, probably forever. The only RYM leader favoring an attempt to fight it out was Jim Mellen, who said:

> PL out-organized us and made us look ridiculous. We were out-organized, out-talked and out-forced, but we can't walk out. We must form a RYM caucus and go back and fight on the basis of ideas.

Eventually RYM leaders decided against Mellen's proposal and began working out plans to make the split formal. About 11:00 that night PL leaders were told RYM was returning to the convention. At 11:30 RYM began filing in, forming a stony-faced ring around the room. Bernardine Dohrn took the microphone and began reading a statement attacking PL for a variety of ideological sins. PL realized what was happening and began to chant, tentatively at first, then more loudly. At 12:15 Sunday morning Bernardine finished reading her statement expelling PL from SDS and then led the RYM people back out of the convention. That night a group of RYM people occupied the national SDS office on West Madison Street, securing control of SDS files, mailing lists and bank accounts. On Sunday RYM met in the First Congregational Church near the headquarters and elected Mark Rudd, Jeff Jones and Bill Ayers as the new national officers. They also elected a new eight-man National Interim Committee. On Monday RYM and PL,

both claiming they were the *real* SDS, held press conferences to give their version of the new situation. Jeff
Jones explained why RYM had "expelled" PL: "It's not
what they say that counts, it's what they do. And what
they have done is in contradiction to what they say."

About a third of the 2000 people attending the convention had walked out with RYM on Friday night, but
the new leaders of SDS felt the gain in organizational
unity was worth the loss in numbers. RYM announced
plans for a national anti-war demonstration in Chicago
in September (the first SDS national action since April,
1965) and for brigades of young Americans to travel to
Cuba to help with the sugar cane harvest.

During the convention Diana was a leading member
of Motor City SDS (which brought seventy people from
Detroit to the convention) and helped organize the Michigan-Ohio axis which sided with RYM. She remained on
the convention floor, chanting and waving a red book
with the rest of Michigan-Ohio SDS. Ayers spent most
of his time with other RYM leaders. Bill and Diana had
begun drifting apart the previous December at the Ann
Arbor NC. They never fought or fell out of love, exactly,
but Ayers insisted his feeling for Diana could not be allowed to limit his freedom or to interfere with his political work. Monogamy, he said, was a bourgeois trait,
one of the things which would go after the revolution.
In 1969 he moved to Chicago to work with the national office on its plans for the recreation of SDS, and
Diana began dividing her time between Ann Arbor and
Motor City SDS in Detroit. Ayers was also spending
more time with Bernardine Dohrn, a good-looking, hard,

highly intelligent girl with a brittle appeal unlike Diana's. The Children's Community School had brought Bill and Diana together; politics separated them.

Early one morning during the convention, probably on Sunday, June 22, after the final walkout, Diana called Karin Rosenberg and asked if she could bring some SDS friends to spend the night. At 4:00 A.M. she finally arrived with a group of seven or eight, who all slept on the floor.

One of the people with Diana that night was Alan Howard, who was covering the SDS convention for Liberation News Service. Before returning to the convention later that day Alan and Diana went out for a long walk down Lake Shore Drive. They talked about the split in SDS and the Weatherman manifesto. Howard had first started Diana thinking in terms of revolution while they were both in Guatemala, but now Diana's commitment had passed his. Howard did not share her belief in the imminence of the world revolution, or that white radicals could appreciably help revolutionaries in other countries by preoccupying the authorities within the United States. He found himself in the awkward position of suggesting that Weatherman was moving too quickly, was isolating itself from the broad classes necessary to give weight to a revolutionary movement. He was, in short, urging caution.

For Diana, however, the revolution had replaced everything else. She rarely saw her family; she had abandoned teaching; she had little in common with her old friends; Bill was drifting away. Politics was Diana's life. Having so little that was her own, she was prepared to give everything for the revolution.

The Violent Summer

THE VICTORY of the Weathermen within SDS was the beginning, not the end, of a series of rapid changes in their sense of themselves as revolutionaries. During the first six months of 1969 the New Left–RYM–Weatherman faction within SDS concerned itself almost exclusively with revolutionary theory; the actions they took were intended to prove the validity of their theory. During the following six months this process was reversed: their emphasis shifted to action and their theorizing was intended only to justify what they had determined to do anyway. Behind this shift in emphasis was a long-suppressed fascination with force and violence, openly indulged only after the expulsion of PL left the new leadership of SDS free of all restraint.

The Weathermen were in love with violence; during that summer they learned to admit their passion. Their arguments all pointed in a single direction: the time had come to fight. The examples of Cuba, where Castro had begun his revolution with 13 men, and of Vietnam, where a nation of 16 million had refused to submit to a nation of 200 million, convinced them that nothing was beyond truly determined men. Nearly 1000 people had walked out of the June convention behind Bernardine Dohrn. If only half of those were prepared to persist until the end, the Weathermen felt they might become the core of a Red Army.

It is difficult to know how well the Weatherman leadership knew its own mind. In their thinking, even when speaking to each other, they may have moved only one step at a time, cautiously avoiding recognition of just where they were heading. If they had been planning to join a religious order they could not have dwelt less on the hardships involved, or more on their own spiritual ecstasy and the moral necessity of what they were about to do. The deciding factor in what happened to SDS was not the small cadre of leaders, who may or may not have fully understood what they were about, but the life of the group as a whole. Its membership was constantly shifting but its direction was unchanging. In 1964 or 1965 someone in SDS declared himself a revolutionary; by 1969 it was impossible for any SDS member to admit he was *not* a revolutionary.

Revolution implies an attack upon the state. Once SDS as an institution, a living organism made up of people, declared itself revolutionary in purpose it created a situation in which some portion of its membership would be always pressing for more militant and resolute action. At some future point SDS would face a choice between abandoning its revolutionary purpose or escalating the struggle to include violence. As Merrill Rosenberg told Diana, revolution means violence and risk, or it is only talk. For SDS the moment of choice arrived in 1969.

The anti-war demonstrations originally called for the weekend of September 27 (later changed to October 8–11 when the first date turned out to conflict with universities on a quarter system) quickly took on form as super-militant, "kick ass" street battles with the police. Weatherman, tired of years of tiptoeing up to society, was going to declare war.

To the vast majority of the radical movement this decision bordered on insanity. The United States was a colossus, and was not about to fall under the attack of five hundred or even a thousand kids, no matter how passionately motivated by revolutionary enthusiasm. After the June convention, Weatherman stopped trying to argue the point. They were going to fight now and those who refused to join them were on the side of the enemy.

Almost as soon as the radical movement came to life in 1960, a child of the civil-rights movement, the question of revolution and of revolutionary violence emerged in the obscure background of public events. The struggles over civil rights for American blacks and over the war in Vietnam were fought out on a stage far wider than that of radical politics, but the radical movement was always close to the center of those larger disputes. The question of violence as a political tool was debated by a small number of people, but that number had a disproportionate influence in the struggle over large issues.

The civil-rights activists who risked, and sometimes lost, their lives in the rural South developed a burning anger for the society which ignored them. Looking back on it, even the most neutral and dispassionate observer must admit their cause was not only just but morally imperative, and their opponents no better than outlaws. For a few brief years, in parts of Mississippi and Alabama, the right was all on one side.

Every faint gain by the movement during that period was paid for in blood, and it was only natural that young black men and women who began by wanting the equal rights accorded them by law, ended by rejecting a society which denied those rights with such brutality. The result was a hate which expressed itself in rich fantasies of retribution. In the fall of 1963, when the white rulers of Mississippi did not hesitate to use violence to maintain their position, black activists in the Student Nonviolent Coordinating Committee (SNCC) talked of beginning a guerrilla war in the Mississippi countryside. They talked about the theories of Mao Tse-tung and Che Guevara, of the black rural population as a sea in which black guerrillas would swim like fish. Sometimes they bought guns, and eventually they announced they were going to start shooting back, but that was as far as the fantasy went.

The reality of Mississippi police and National Guardsmen could not be ignored, and the limited gains of the civil-rights movement were nonetheless steady and real. As the pace of change gradually increased, SNCC's anger became a crippling obstacle. It faded away as an organization, still talking guns and black power, while local organizations with concrete aims took over the movement.

The fantasy of revolutionary violence in America did not disappear, however. Movement thinking was always rapid. The desire for reform became a desire for fundamental and finally for revolutionary change before American society could bring itself to act on the original demands for reform. The student movement was uninterrupted in its drift to the left. Activists became socialists and then revolutionaries and learned to accept the idea of revolutionary violence while continuing to recognize the realities of American society. They wanted a revolution, and their anger made them want the violence which came with it, but revolution in America seemed out of the question.

In December, 1964, a group of black militants met with Che Guevara at the Hotel Theresa in Harlem during a visit to the United Nations by Fidel Castro. The militants asked Che what he thought of the possibilities for guerrilla war in the United States. "Here?" said Che, astounded. "I speak not out of sympathy with your government, but out of reality when I tell you not to try guerrilla warfare in this country."

When white movement-activists shifted their attention from the civil-rights movement to the war in Vietnam early in 1965, the revolutionary strain within the radical movement began to predominate. The violence used by the United States against Vietnam seemed to justify violence in return. The problem, as usual, was that no one could demonstrate the sense in revolutionary violence. By the summer of 1967, when black ghettos erupted into open rebellion in cities across the country, a growing segment of the SDS national leadership was emotionally committed to revolution and was seeking ways to justify violence as a practical means of pursuing that goal.

The question of armed struggle was debated endlessly that summer and fall in SDS's Chicago headquarters. Eric Mann, half-convinced — against his better judgment — that white radicals might fight as guerrillas alongside blacks in future riots, proposed the idea to a black leader in Newark where he had worked with the Community Union Project. "Mann, what the fuck are you talking about?" the black leader exploded. "We don't want to shoot it out. If there's another riot it'll be a blood bath for our people. We need guns to protect ourselves. We may even have to use a little sabotage in the right places. But we're interested in building political power. Guns just aren't where it's at." Mann felt like a fool for even proposing the idea.

Revolution in America was a fantasy not only because it was fantastic, but because white radicals literally daydreamed about it. More than a few of them began novels about young Americans who join Latin American revolutionaries in the mountains or take to the wilderness in the United States. This recurring fantasy partly explains the attachment of white radicals to the Black Panthers. The notion that guerrilla war could be carried out only in the countryside was disproved by the failure of Che in the Bolivian mountains and the relative success of urban guerrillas in Uruguay, Guatemala and Brazil. White radicals felt it was conceivable that Black Panthers might win control of black ghettos through urban guerrilla warfare, a notion the Panthers also entertained, but never attempted to implement.

The fantasy of violence was joined with another strand of the radical movement in America: an existential emphasis on personal authenticity as a criterion of valid politics. White movement-activists became revolutionaries because they had emotionally rejected American society. Revolutionary ambitions might be impractical, but they were more honest than compromise. They looked for a kind of spiritual purity in politics. They rejected the materialism which they felt had corrupted American society. Eventually, they were as much drawn to revolution for what it would destroy as for what it would create.

Revolution reflected a taste for absolutism almost religious in its intensity. Just as Jesuits make vows of poverty, chastity and obedience not for the good it will do the world, but for the good it will do them, so white radicals rejected the world around them and dedicated themselves to an order aimed at its overthrow. Pure in their aims (nothing for *them*), they tended to judge each other by the totality and selflessness of their commitment. Middle-class in origin, white radicals were sensitive to the charge that they could drop out of the movement at any moment and resume the protected, privileged lives they had left behind.

Realizing this, and perhaps defensive about their own revolutionary inertia, black militants took a certain pleas-

ure in attacking white radicals as summertime soldiers
playing at revolution. An example of this, and of its effect, occurred at Columbia University early in the morning of April 24, 1968. The previous day Mark Rudd had
led Columbia SDS into an administration building to protest (among other things) the building of a gymnasium
in a Harlem park. Because the gymnasium primarily
affected the black community, black student organizations
were forced to join SDS in the occupation. That night,
however, the blacks ordered Rudd and the other whites
to leave the building.

Later, after the whites had occupied a second building, Rudd told other SDS leaders why he had surrendered
to the blacks' demand. "The reason we were asked to
leave Hamilton (the occupied building) was because we
weren't solid," Rudd said. "I didn't want to tell you this
before, but the blacks have guns and are prepared to make
a stand. I'm not." He hesitated while his words were ab-
sorbed by the others. "I'm not ready to sacrifice my life.
There are still things I want to accomplish and I didn't
want any of my people to get hurt. That's their fight, we
have our own. For some of us our academic careers are
already ruined. The only thing we can do is make our
stand and try to win our fight. I didn't want to leave Dean
(Henry) Coleman there with guns and all that in the
building, but I had no choice." *

It was an emotional moment. Some of those present
cried. Rudd's nerve had failed; he knew it, and every-

---

* This quote is from Jerry L. Avorn, *Up Against the Ivy Wall* (New
York: Atheneum, 1969), p. 65.

one else knew it. After that, he always chose the most militant path as if proving that now, at least, he was willing to make any sacrifice. Whatever his later failings, Rudd never again retreated from a situation out of fear. As a leader of the Weathermen he insisted in speech after speech on the importance of personal courage and of exorcising the fear of violence, of being ready not only to suffer physical pain, but to inflict it. He was not talking about dying in some future revolutionary apocalypse; he was talking about dying *right now.*

These three strands — the politics of personal authenticity, Rudd's emphasis on physical courage, and the longstanding fantasies of violent revolution in America — came together in Weatherman. The only way to exorcise their fear, to prove their courage and commitment, was to act, whether or not it made conventional political sense. They argued that an attack on the state was morally necessary. Once convinced of its necessity, the utility of such an attack became irrelevant.

Throughout the summer and early fall of 1969 everything the Weathermen did was designed to steel themselves for a pure act of the will. In Jim Mellen's phrase, they were to become the "tools of necessity," the agents of history. They sometimes joked about "Mellen's Hegel rap," but they took it seriously. They were going to surrender themselves to history, to make themselves into history's cutting edge, to become the catalyst of historical change.

The inevitability of their destruction gave a passionate air, half gay and half savage, to everything they did. They did not underestimate the situation which faced them.

They knew they were placing themselves between the ax and the tree, and yet they were determined to go ahead anyway. Bill Ayers was always talking about politics that were "real," by which he meant politics that had an immediate effect on people's lives. For the Weathermen, violence, long an abstract notion, became real as soon as the June convention came to an end.

Bill and Diana saw little of each other during the summer of 1969. As the new education secretary of SDS, Ayers left Chicago for Boston to attend a meeting of the New England SDS the first week in July. PL, always strong in New England, insisted on its right to attend the meeting and a fistfight erupted which foreshadowed a summer of violent battles between the two factions. Later in July, Bill and the other leaders of RYM went to Oakland, California, to attend a conference called by the Black Panthers to establish a United Front Against Fascism.

For the Weathermen, the conference was the beginning of open warfare against PL. One night during an SDS caucus more than a hundred Weathermen filed out of the room for a raid on PL. On Saturday, July 19, Weathermen physically removed PL people who insisted on handing out leaflets critical of the Panthers. The following morning, when PL returned, a fight erupted in which ten PLers were beaten badly enough to require hospital treatment. The Berkeley Radical Student Union, made up of former SDSers who had left the Berkeley chapter after it was taken over by PL and who had been RYM allies at the June convention, denounced the attacks on PL, but the Weathermen shrugged off the criticism.

The taste for violence also created a new split within the

SDS National Interim Committee. Mike Klonsky and Bob Avakian of the Bay Area Revolutionary Union (BARU), both members of the NIC, broke with Weatherman at an NIC meeting following the Oakland conference. "You guys aren't into serving the people, you're into fighting the people," they said.

The Weathermen dismissed that attack, too, denouncing the issue-oriented politics of Klonsky and Avakian as "serve the people shit." They meant that fighting for piecemeal gains was a form of *economism,* a surrender of revolutionary aims in order to win limited goals. One of the NIC members, Barbara Reilly (a German girl who had been close to Rudd at Columbia), had already resigned and been replaced by Phoebe Hirsch. When planning for the October national action became steadily more militant, Klonsky and Avakian resigned, too, forming a new SDS faction called Revolutionary Youth Movement II, which made plans for its own actions in Chicago on October 8–11. RYM I, as it was sometimes called, began referring to itself as Weatherman.

Diana, meanwhile, had been chosen as part of an SDS-controlled delegation to a meeting in Cuba with representatives of North Vietnam and of the Provisional Revolutionary Government of South Vietnam. The meeting was the third between Vietnamese and representatives of the American radical movement, the others having taken place in Bratislava, Czechoslovakia, in the summer of 1967, and in Budapest in the summer of 1968. The prominent role played by SDS in the 1969 meeting was a reflection of the group's passionate conversion to internationalism. Beginning with the victory of Weatherman in SDS, the organization saw itself as part of a worldwide movement rather than a group with aims limited to the United States.

Early in July, while Bill was in Boston, Diana and four other Weathermen met in the SDS national headquarters for a briefing on the meeting with the Vietnamese by a member of Columbia SDS who had accompanied Bernardine Dohrn to Budapest the previous summer. The thirty-six-member delegation, leaving from a number of cities inside the United States, traveled quietly to avoid the attention of the FBI. Their airline tickets to Mexico City had been purchased from a Scarsdale, New York, travel agent who kept wondering why the group would need no return tickets. The delegation, which included Ted Gold and Kathy Boudin, spent nearly five weeks in Cuba, including two weeks with the seven-member delegations from North and South Vietnam.

The Vietnamese had called the meeting to ask pointedly where the American peace movement was now that the war in Vietnam was entering its final stages. The SDS, which had abandoned the anti-war movement after staging a single demonstration in April, 1965, had a bad conscience on this subject and insisted on the strength of its new commitment.

The Vietnamese spent eight full days on detailed briefings explaining how and why the United States faced defeat in Vietnam. "The greatest invention of the twentieth century has not been nuclear weapons, but people's war," said a member of the Vietnamese People's Liberation Armed Forces. "The United States can never escape from the labyrinth and sea of fire of people's war."

With its characteristic enthusiam, Weatherman tended

to exaggerate the imminence of the American defeat in
Vietnam. The Vietnamese insisted that defeat was inevitable; the Weathermen allowed themselves to believe it
might be coming that fall. They also tended to exaggerate
the imminence of guerrilla risings in Latin America and,
of all places, even in South Korea (apparently because
the North Korean leader, Kim II Sung, said so. They
made no allowance for exaggeration on his part.) The
defeat of American imperialism might not be a generation
away, they felt, but literally around the corner.

They began to feel that history was escalating, that the
rise of blacks in the United States and the defeat of Americans abroad might occur even before they had a chance
to play their part in the revolution. Doubt and caution
had not characterized their expulsion of PL or their plans
for Chicago in October. Every impression in Cuba seemed
to confirm their excited sense that the revolution was coming *now*.

While the American delegation met as a whole with the
Vietnamese, factions within the delegation also had private meetings with them. Making up the American group
were fifteen SDSers (only two of them from the RYM II
faction), nine Latin Americans from New York and Chicago, two members of New York's High School Student
Union (HSSU), and a number of radical journalists and
other unaffiliated individuals. The split taking place
within SDS back in the United States was reflected in the
Cuba delegation, Weathermen on one side and the HSSU,
the Latins, and the RYM II people on the other.

Diana, who was having a brief but intense affair with

one of the Latins, was to some extent caught in the middle, but managed to avoid a situation in which she was forced to choose between them. This was characteristic of the relationship between Bill and Diana. Her affair on the trip to Cuba did not reflect upon her primary allegiance to Bill. His adventures on the side implied little about his feelings for her. While he was in the SDS headquarters and living with the national collective that summer and fall, Bill always kept a picture of Diana on his desk.

During the private meetings in Cuba the Vietnamese tended to encourage the Americans in whichever direction they were naturally inclined to move. They told the RYM II people that mass demonstrations were a useful tactic at the same time that they were encouraging the Weathermen to try street fighting. This apparent contradiction was the result of a Vietnamese sense that everything helped, but it caused confusion after the delegation returned to the United States. In America the Weathermen said they had been told by Van Ba, "When you go into a city, look for the person who fights hardest against the cops. That's the one you talk all night with. Don't look for the one who says the best thing. Look for the one who fights."

Typically, Diana's family did not know she was in Cuba until shortly before her return. They found out only after Mrs. Oughton's mother died and Diana's signature was needed on some papers concerning the will. (Diana had once so alarmed Mrs. Oughton's mother about the younger generation that she left nothing to any of her grandchildren.) Carol suggested that her mother call Bill

Ayers at SDS headquarters in Chicago, since he always knew where Diana was. When Mrs. Oughton finally reached him, he told her Diana was in Cuba.

Back in the United States the Weathermen were already putting Van Ba's advice into practice. With every passing week Weatherman militance increased in its intensity. Their plans for the Chicago demonstration called for the opening battle in a revolutionary war. At a meeting of the Detroit anti-war movement in the Central Methodist Church on July 21, 1969, Motor City SDS frightened more moderate groups with their explanation of what was going to happen in Chicago. "We're not going to Chicago to get our ass kicked," they said; "we're going to kick ass."

Motor City SDS had begun the summer with demonstrations at Detroit movie theaters showing the movie *Che!* When the lights went up between shows Weathermen would take the stage and begin talking about the issues of economic imperialism so notably missing from the movie. By the meeting of July 21 they had adopted a theory of organizing by assault.

One Saturday afternoon in the middle of July about forty members of Motor City SDS had gone to Detroit's Metropolitan Beach, known as Metro Beach by the white working-class youths who spent weekends there. The Weathermen, forming ranks around a member carrying a red flag, marched from one end of the beach to the other handing out leaflets. At the end of their sweep they planted the flag in the midst of a crowd and began to argue aggressively with the white youths, many of them Vietnam veterans, who gathered around. At one point an angry veteran said, "Let's get the flag," and a general brawl erupted. Someone suddenly shouted the police were on their way and Motor City SDS retreated — so abruptly, in fact, that several members were left behind in the middle of the hostile crowd.

The theory behind the Metro Beach riot, as Motor City SDS proudly explained it, was that working-class kids were turned off by sissy intellectuals who talked about fighting the ruling class but always had some smooth reason why the actual moment to fight had not quite arrived. By openly proclaiming their commitment to communism, and by proving their commitment by fighting, the Weathermen would win the respect of working-class kids. A punch in the nose, properly explained, would do more to radicalize the grease (as working-class kids were called) than years of patient explanation.

"It was great," Bill told one friend about the Metro Beach riot. "We're communists and we're calling ourselves communists. The kids love it."

Motor City SDS also invaded a White Castle hamburger drive-in on weekend nights to hand out leaflets about the Days of Rage among the crowd of several hundred teen-agers always hanging around. They came back again and again, sometimes getting in fights, rapping about the revolution, eluding the police, and inviting the kids to SDS meetings held every Monday night at St. Joseph's Church in Detroit. The leaflet which most alarmed the rest of the radical and peace movements in Detroit was one which stridently declared, "The war's on and everybody's got to take sides!" It went on to say, in the exaggeratedly crude language affected by the Weathermen:

> The thing is this: the Man can't fight everywhere. He
> can't even beat the Vietnamese. And when other Viet-
> nams start, man, he's just gonna fall apart. SDS is re-
> cruiting an army right now, man, a *people's* army, under
> black leadership, that's gonna fight against the pigs and
> win!!!

The Motor City SDS version of what was going to
happen in Chicago in October seemed like the wildest sort
of irresponsible adventurism. The *Fifth Estate*, a Detroit
underground paper whose commitment to revolution
could not be faulted, wrote an open letter to the Weatherman leadership criticizing plans for the Chicago action.
The only effect, the paper argued, would be a storm of
repression, of which there was already more than enough.
Because their attack was symptomatic of the reaction of
movement people everywhere, Weatherman replied in a
long letter published in the following issue (August 21–
September 3):

> It is arrogant for white mothercountry revolutionaries to
> talk about holding back the struggle for a better day,
> while the Vietnamese and other Third World peoples are
> facing genocide daily. There has not been in recent years,
> nor can we imagine, a single instance of fighting too hard
> to destroy imperialism . . .

> We don't really believe we can stop the trial [of the
> Chicago 8, one of the nominal issues of the Days of Rage]
> but our intention to try and make the rulers pay a price
> for holding such an event should be as clear now as it was

in Chicago last summer or in Oakland [during a week of antidraft street actions] in 1967.

Weatherman admitted the demonstration would be violent, but denied that it would be adventurist. They might not be able to do much to hurt imperial America, they said, but every little bit helps. The United States was already totally opposed to the world revolution; therefore, nothing the Weathermen could do would make it more opposed.

In planning for the Days of Rage Weatherman seriously considered the possibility of a wholesale massacre by police, but finally ruled it out. If there were ten or fifteen dead that would be a victory, proving their commitment. Besides, they said, white radicals were no better than Vietcong peasants, who had been dying by the thousands for years. Excessive fear of the consequences of the Days of Rage, like that expressed by the *Fifth Estate*, was itself a form of racism. Revolutionaries had to be both ready to die and ready to kill.

The Weathermen hoped that creating an image of strength and determination would win converts to revolutionary violence. In their minds the moral and political issues had all been settled long ago; America was racist, oppressive and corrupt, and violent overthrow was the only solution. The Weathermen felt that these were self-evident truths and that people would make the right choice if they were confronted with a situation they could not avoid. Timidity and defeatism had prevented movement people from attempting to overthrow the system in the past, but now Vietnam had shown America was not invincible.

The revolutionary practice which emerged from Weatherman theory was little more than ideological gangsterism, isolating Weatherman on the left without recruiting anyone. In a typical action 10 Weatherwomen invaded a social science class at Macomb Community College outside Detroit on Thursday, July 31. Interrupting a final exam being taken by 35 students, the women began a twenty-minute harangue about imperialism and women's liberation, handing out a pamphlet on "SDS Women Fighters" and talking about the Chicago action scheduled for October. When two men tried to protest they were subdued with karate the women had been practicing in their collectives. The women's vigilance faltered, however, and the instructor managed to slip out a back door. As the women were leaving the college grounds a few minutes later police arrived and arrested nine of them, who were immediately elevated by SDS to the status of political prisoners as the Motor City 9. When the SDS tried to raise bail money in Detroit's radical community they met nothing but refusals; movement people were not really sure they wanted Weatherpeople loose on the streets.

There were four Weatherman collectives active in Detroit that summer, with a total membership of 35 or 40. Perhaps as many more could be expected to show up at SDS rallies and demonstrations. The Monday night meetings in St. Joseph's Church drew up to 80 curious teenagers, but usually fewer. Nevertheless, Motor City SDS hoped that at least 1000 Detroit greasers would show up in Chicago to fight the police on Wednesday, October 8. Other Weatherman collectives in Cleveland, Columbus, Boulder, Boston, New York and several other cities carried out similar actions, equally exhilarating, and equally unsuccessful.

In the middle of August Bill Ayers and several other Weathermen from the national headquarters, now renamed the Weather Bureau, went to St. John's, Canada, to meet the SDS delegation returning from Cuba by boat. On August 29, Bill, Diana and about 300 other Weathermen from around the country went to Cleveland for a four-day Midwest National Action Conference held in the East Cleveland Congregational Church. The meeting, closed to the traditional press and only sketchily reported in underground newspapers, was dominated by the question of the role of women in the movement, beginning with a "Free Ahmed Evans" demonstration by 12 Weatherwomen on the steps of Cleveland's Union Club.

The group quickly divided into men's and women's caucuses to debate the question of monogamy. Women argued that couples in love tended to defend each other in criticism sessions and that loyalty to an individual inevitably drained one's commitment to the revolution. They insisted that monogamy be outlawed in Weatherman collectives. When Mike Klonsky tried to defend monogamy the women shouted him down, chanting, "Running dog, run away." Eric Mann also favored monogamy but went along in the end.

Diana and Bill had long had an understanding which

limited their commitment to each other, but now they faced separation as a matter of political principle. Diana had always believed that she and Bill would end up together but, in a speech which summed up the feeling and thinking of Weatherman as an organization, Bill seemed to close the door forever on that possibility:

> We have one task, and that's to make ourselves into tools of the revolution . . .
>
> Any notion that people can have a primary responsibility for one person, that they can have that "out" — we have to destroy that notion in order to build a collective, we have to destroy all "outs" to destroy the notion that people can lean on one person and not be responsible to the entire collective.

Ayers made it clear that things would get harder, not easier, now that Weatherman had decided to fight. The Weathermen would have to be strong, to remember that they could win no matter how overwhelming the odds might at first appear:

> You join the movement because you want to be part of that worldwide struggle that's obviously winning, and you win people over to it, and you win people over by being honest to them about the risks, by being honest to them about the struggle, by being honest to them that what they are getting into is a fight. It's not a comfortable life, it's not just a dollar more, it's standing up in the face of the enemy, and risking your life and risking everything for that struggle . . .
>
> We have to deal with the fact that in a lot of ways all of

us have elements of defeatism in us, and don't really believe we can win, don't really believe that the United
States can be beaten. But we have to believe it, because
defeatism is based on individualism . . . and we have to
beat that attitude out of ourselves.

The struggle began immediately. Movement people
later joked that there were 300 "divorces" in Cleveland
that weekend. Most of them separated casual couples,
but a number of them were real divorces, breaking up
perfectly healthy marriages. In several instances children, too, were given up for the revolution.

During the conference people were arbitrarily picked
for "trashing," exaggeratedly brutal criticism by the entire
group. Others were picked out for exaggerated praise.
Every remark was subject to the most minute analysis.
Every action, every facial expression, was assumed to have
a political content. One was responsible for everything.
Adopted from Maoist political theory, life in the collectives which Weatherman was creating was to be dominated by three slogans:

CRITICISM—SELF-CRITICISM—TRANSFORMATION
POLITICS IN COMMAND
EVERYTHING FOR THE REVOLUTION

Everything
for the Revolution

DIANA'S LIFE NOW ENTERED a new phase in which everything was subordinate to the will of others. From the time the Cleveland conference ended on Monday, September 1, her life was to be fighting; brutal emotional collisions within collectives; suppression of her love for Bill Ayers; an attempt to root out the gentle qualities which were considered part of her bourgeois background, rather than part of her nature.

That week she and 75 other Weatherwomen drove to Pittsburgh for an exemplary action intended as a practice run for Chicago. On Wednesday, September 3, the group made contact with the SDS chapter at the University of Pittsburgh and attacked it for sticking to campus-oriented issues instead of moving out into the city to create a revolutionary "Steel City SDS." They also contacted the local American Friends Service Committee to ask if they could use the committee's mimeograph machine. The AFSC turned them down.

The following morning, on Thursday, September 4, 20 Weatherwomen invaded the AFSC office and held the office workers captive while they ran off a leaflet. At 12:30 P.M. all 75 Weatherwomen suddenly appeared on the grounds of South Hills High School while about a third of the school's 2000 students were outside on their lunch break. The Weatherwomen spray-painted "Ho Lives" and "Free Huey" on the school's main entrance doors and then charged inside shouting "Jailbreak!" and "Shut down the school!" A student ran to the cafeteria to warn Vice Principal Alfred R. Fascetti what was happening. He left his table and went out into the hall where he was met by 40 screaming women, at least one of them (he said later in court) with her breasts exposed. "What the hell are you doing in this school?" he shouted. His only answer was a storm of abuse.

The women handed out leaflets in the schoolyard, made speeches about imperialism, racism and the SDS national action in Chicago, and then began to leave the school grounds. At this point the Pittsburgh police arrived and started to arrest the women, who astonished them by fighting to get free.

Diana was one of those who managed to escape, but 26 others were arrested, including Cathy Wilkerson and Jane Spielman. The high-school students had been mystified by the raid; they had no idea who the Weatherwomen were or why their school was being invaded. School officials were doubly mystified. The courts let the Weatherwomen know they took the matter seriously by imposing $1500 bail each on 24 of the women and $10,000 each on two of them, a total of $56,000.

The following day, while Diana and the other women were on their way back to Chicago, Diana's sister Pam, who was to be married on Saturday, repeatedly called the SDS national headquarters to ask where Diana was. After being brushed off a number of times she went down to the office on West Madison Street but was turned away at the door. On Saturday morning Diana finally called her family in Dwight and told them she had an important meeting and could not make the wedding. "My life isn't my own," she told Pam. "I don't make the decisions about how I use my time."

Pam, who had been counting on Diana's presence, burst into tears. When the family left Dwight for the Chicago church where the wedding was to take place, Diana's bridesmaid's dress was still at home across her bed. (Despite her absence she was listed among the wedding party in an account of the wedding published in the Dwight *Star and Herald* the following week.)

Shortly after the Pittsburgh raid Diana and some other members of Motor City SDS moved to Flint, Michigan, an industrial city north of Detroit, where they established a Weatherman collective at 915 East Fourth Avenue. During the next four months Diana spent most of her time in collectives in Flint and Detroit, her life dominated by the attempt to destroy everything she had been in order to recreate herself as a disciplined, single-minded revolutionary. During the six weeks between the Cleveland conference and the Four Days of Rage in October, life in the collectives took on a frenzied, brutal, savage air as the Weathermen tried to root out their fear of violence, their sexual inhibitions, their sense of themselves as individuals and all their "bourgeois hangups" about privacy, cleanliness, politeness, tolerance and humor.

Weatherman felt that movement people had failed in the past because they were not totally dedicated to the revolution. They intended to exorcise every error in thinking, feeling or behavior: CRITICISM–SELF-CRITICISM–TRANSFORMATION. In practice this meant long meetings in which individuals would analyze themselves for deviation from correct thinking or for mistakes in their practice. The self-criticism would be followed by criticism of the individual by the group, an often cruel process. On the basis of criticism and self-criticism the individual was expected to transform himself.

The purpose of this self-transformation was to end their sense of themselves as private individuals with private lives, and to make themselves into "tools of the revolution." Every action, every thought, every word was to be judged only by its political utility: POLITICS IN COMMAND. Every personal resource, spiritual, physical and financial, was to be devoted to the cause: EVERYTHING FOR THE REVOLUTION.

Daily life in the communes centered on criticism sessions, karate and rifle practice, and political actions designed to sharpen the members' ability to behave as a coherent group. In practice EVERYTHING FOR THE REVOLUTION meant nothing for anything else. As a result, the collectives turned into foul sties where beds went unmade, food rotted on unwashed plates, toilets jammed, dirty clothes piled up in corners.

The emotional atmosphere inside the collectives, barricaded behind windows covered with chicken wire (to keep out bombs) and double-locked doors (to keep out police), was savage and neurotic. On one occasion Diana's collective killed, cooked and ate a tomcat. On another, they went on a tombstone-smashing rampage through a local graveyard.

The smashing of monogamy meant, in practice, communal sexual relations. In some instances homosexuality and lesbianism were involved, occasionally by order of the collective when it was thought an individual was not being honest about latent sexual tendencies. Some collectives even planned to raise money by prostitution, both male and female.

Most of the time alcohol, tobacco and drugs were forbidden, but during one period collectives took LSD together, on direct orders from the Weather Bureau in Chicago, for the double purpose of breaking down their old sense of themselves as individuals (an effect often reported by LSD converts) and of weeding out suspected police informers.

Every expenditure was a matter for group decision and Diana's dividend checks went into the common fund, as did all other monies. Collectives imposed foodless days on themselves when they needed to save money for bail or other purposes. Sometimes they stayed awake for two- and three-day periods in order to discipline themselves for the hardships they would face as members of the Red Army.

Inside the collectives the Weathermen were cruel to themselves and each other. Hurt feelings and smoldering grudges poisoned the atmosphere; suffering themselves, people tended to attack each other with increasing violence. Individuals were sometimes attacked so brutally in group criticism sessions they were left whimpering and speechless. Individuals who seemed to hold back some part of themselves were subject to harsh psychological assault; if they persisted, they were sometimes purged. Everyone was overtired and underfed, nervous and fearful. People became stiff and unnatural, afraid they would be attacked for the slightest error, a deliberate process which sometimes hid a desire literally to *destroy.*

Diana, naturally gentle, was often criticized for her reluctance to accept violence and sexuality divorced from love. She admitted that violence was necessary, that sexuality might be good in itself, but she found it hard to live by those principles. Her balance and moderation helped to prevent the excesses that took place in some collectives, but only at great cost to herself. It was often Diana who pressed for a rest during long, highly charged meetings; the others, anxious to avoid showing the slightest sign of weakness, did not always thank her for it. When Diana was insufficiently militant during Weatherman actions, and especially after she quietly talked politics with a policeman who arrested her during a raid on Flint's Central High School on September 22, Diana was the victim of concentrated attack. "You're a revolutionary now, not a society bitch," one Weatherman shouted at her. Nevertheless, she continued to defend what she felt was right. It was this quality of strength which explains the position Diana held in the Jesse James Gang, SDS and Weatherman.

She was never a leader in the traditional sense; during three years she was quoted in an underground paper only once (in the *Fifth Estate* following the June, 1969, convention). She lived by her political principles, however, and gave other people confidence that they could do the same. She never seemed to forget the purpose of all their political activity, and in this way constantly reminded others they were out to create something new, not solely to destroy the old. Few knew Diana other than her friends, but her friends included the leaders of Weatherman and she was close to the center of Weatherman thinking until the end.

On September 27 Diana and two other members of the Flint collective, John Pilkington and David Chase (who had also been arrested on the twenty-second in Flint), drove to Detroit for a Michigan SDS rally outside the city's public library which, like the Pittsburgh high-school raid, was intended as practice for the Days of Rage. The rally, nominally aimed at war research by members of the Wayne State University faculty, began on the steps of the main library about 1:30 P.M. An hour later John Jacobs, carrying a red flag, led a march down Woodward in the general direction of a WSU research center. Jacobs suddenly swerved into the middle of the street, followed by 60 Weathermen who blocked traffic. A dozen police moved into the crowd to arrest Jacobs (who was charged with anarchy, a felony on the basis of an old law about red flags) and the mass of marchers started to run down a side street, the police in hot pursuit. Moments later, however, the Weathermen abruptly turned and attacked the police, who were not only outnumbered but astounded.

During the brief struggle Diana was one of eight women who dragged down a policeman, allowing a ninth to free herself. Besides Jacobs, nine other Weathermen were arrested during the action, including Chase and Pilkington, who was cornered by six police in the driveway of Detroit's Orthopedic Hospital and severely beaten.

Early in October Diana and Bill Ayers returned to Ann Arbor to recruit for the Days of Rage. In a meeting held at Canterbury House, a religious center for students, Diana talked about her discussions with the Vietnamese in Cuba, quoting Van Ba's advice about organizing. Members of the audience, which included people who had once belonged to the James Gang, attacked her as a liar, quoting contradictory statements made by the Vietnamese to other factions on the Cuba trip.

Ayers also spoke at the meeting, arguing that Weatherman's summer-long organizing was beginning to pay off and predicting that at least 1000 working-class teen-agers, tough grease thinking in political terms for the first time, would join Motor City SDS for the Days of Rage.

"When I was at Ann Arbor all the talk about revolution was in the abstract," Ayers told the hostile audience. "Since we've moved to Detroit we've made the revolution real. The grease come up to us and say, 'Hey, aren't you the guys who beat up the pigs at McDonald's [a chain of hamburger drive-ins] last night? How come?"

"You understand the revolution when you make the revolution, not when you talk about it. If I'm going into a new town I don't look for the guy with a comprehensive political analysis, I look for the kids who are fighting the pigs."

The hostility encountered by Bill and Diana in Ann Arbor was the rule, not the exception. Weatherman's strongarm recruiting tactics, predicated on the notion of confronting people with their reactionary beliefs, had succeeded only in antagonizing the vast majority of the radical movement. When SDS people abandoned traditional parliamentary procedures in late 1968 and began heckling at meetings and physically threatening their opponents they made sudden political gains, taking over campus SDS chapters, capturing public attention and creating an image of dramatic forward movement. The image, however, was largely an illusion. Their ruthlessness inevitably alienated former movement allies who eventually turned their accumulated anger against Weatherman.

At the Panther conference on creating a United Front Against Fascism in July, SDS had been strongly criticized by old allies for its preoccupation with trashing PL. A few weeks later the ranking Panther official neither in jail nor in exile, David Hilliard, threatened SDS with physical violence in an interview with the Berkeley *Barb*. When the *Guardian* reported on the dispute at length, Mark Rudd made matters worse by angrily accusing the paper of counter-revolutionary tendencies no less pronounced than those of *Time* magazine. The *Guardian*, naturally, became an enemy of Weatherman, rather than simply an opponent.

Weatherman's aggressiveness evoked similar responses elsewhere. On August 9, the twenty-fourth anniversary of the Hiroshima bomb, Jeff Jones, one of the three national officers elected at the June convention, spoke at an anti-war rally in New York's Central Park, where every political splinter in the city was in a bickering mood. He managed to anger all of them, denouncing them in turn for not being sufficiently anti-imperialist.

At the University of Wisconsin in Madison in September, Jones and a dozen other Weathermen, including one of the celebrated Motor City 9, broke into a regular SDS organizational meeting to harangue the group about the Days of Rage. Grabbing the microphone while the other Weathermen surrounded him, glaring fiercely out at the crowd, Jones denounced them all for a host of political sins, of which the most prominent was unwillingness to join Weatherman in Chicago. They were objectively racist, he shouted, because they were relying on their white-skin privilege by remaining in a protected university atmosphere. "None of us go to any motherfucking university," Jones said.

"Yeah, y'all graduated," someone in the audience shouted back.

The self-consciously ferocious style affected by the Weathermen, the boots and dirty dungarees and leather jackets, their crude language (a wildly inaccurate imitation of the language of working-class kids), their arrogant insistence that the rest of the movement must fall in line *or else,* only angered most radicals over the age of sixteen. At the University of Wisconsin one radical dismissed the Weathermen in a widely quoted remark: "You don't need a rectal thermometer," he said, "to know who the assholes are."

Mark Rudd fared little better in his recruiting appearances. When he spoke at the U.S. Student Press Association Conference in Boulder, Colorado, in August, flanked by two Weatherwomen allegedly trained in karate, most of the college and high-school editors considered him a revolutionary buffoon. On September 25 Rudd appeared at City College in New York, a welt under one eye left from the beating he had received at a McDonald's drive-in in Milwaukee. Rudd's militance left the students unmoved.

The following day he went to Boston and told a crowd in Boston University's Haydn Hall, "You're fools if you don't get guns and join the revolution." The audience was more impressed by the behavior of local Weathermen who had beaten up a couple of people in a raid on Harvard University's Center for International Affairs the day before. They acted as bodyguards during Rudd's appearance, searching everyone who came in the room, especially the women, and brutally beating an obviously feebleminded youth discovered with a can of Mace. While the audience sat in sickened silence, the beating went on and on. The young man was finally dragged off insensible. No one in Boston was recruited for Weatherman's revolution.

In this violent atmosphere friends turned against each other. SDS people who planned to stay home in October were subjected to violent emotional pressure from old allies. Weathermen were, of course, right in thinking the revolution might begin if everyone went to Chicago; they were wrong in thinking there was any way of getting everyone to go.

As the day approached their recruiting attempts became increasingly violent; they were publicly confident, privately desperate. Nothing worked. SDS chapters from New York to Oregon voted against taking any part in the national action scheduled for October 8–11. They sided with the Fayetteville, Arkansas, chapter which issued a widely reprinted statement in August dissociating itself with both Weatherman and PL. "All power to the people," the statement ended; "No power to the Stalinists."

In New York veterans of Columbia SDS who had once worked beside Rudd, John Jacobs and other Weathermen, deliberately rescheduled a demonstration at Fort Dix, New Jersey, so it would conflict with the Days of Rage and keep movement people away from Chicago. At the same time Liberation News Service, which had once considered itself the propaganda arm of SDS, refused to print a Weatherman pamphlet unless the Weather Bureau began genuinely cooperating with former SDS allies like the Black Panthers and the Young Lords of Chicago. (Weatherman made a feeble gesture in this direction, establishing a relationship with Youth Against War and Fascism in which YAWF helped Weatherman with organizational details and Weatherman began publishing stories about YAWF's favorite political prisoner, Martin Sostre, in *New Left Notes*.)

During the final six weeks before the Days of Rage,

Weatherman collectives tried to build support for the action by high-school raids, especially in Detroit and Boston. At the same time Weatherman leaders spoke at colleges and universities where SDS had traditionally been strong, insisting that *now* was the time to choose sides. The cadre in the Weatherman collectives probably numbered between 300 and 400, but the Weather Bureau always expected far more than that small number to show up in Chicago's Lincoln Park on the night of October 8, the second anniversary of the death of Che Guevara.

In a moment of enthusiasm one Weatherman leader predicted, early in September, that 50,000 to 100,000 movement people and high-school grease would show up for the Days of Rage. As the day approached, however, more levelheaded Weathermen publicly predicted 10,000, hoped for 5000 and truly expected no less than 2500. Even the lower figure, they felt, would be enough to bust up "Pig City." As a gesture of good luck on Monday night, October 6, Weathermen dynamited the statue commemorating seven policemen killed by a bomb during a rally in Haymarket Square during the 1880s.

On October 7, it began to be apparent that the Weather Bureau had been living a dream. In New York less than half those who had promised to come actually appeared when the chartered buses began to load for Chicago. In Boston, Cleveland, Boulder and Detroit, the centers of Weatherman strength, the situation was the same.

When Weatherpeople began collecting at the park Wednesday night, helmets, clubs and chains hidden in paper sacks, they momentarily lost heart as they surveyed the tiny crowd, at least half of it reporters and bystanders. A fire was built from park benches and Weather leaders began making speeches about Che Guevara and white-skin privilege and the world revolution and why it was necessary to do as they were about to do. The final speech ended with a call to head for the Drake Hotel, where Federal Judge Julius Hoffman, presiding at the trial of the Chicago 8, lived in solitary elegance.

No more than 300 strong, the Weathermen moved out of the park and into the streets. They pulled out their clubs and chains and began smashing car windshields and plateglass windows. The surprised police moved aside or were overrun. In the first minutes the Weathermen attacked a number of police and a few passersby, including an acquaintance of Diana's father, a former Harvard football player who lived along the route of march. The man thought the sound of shattering glass was the work of vandals and he came down from his apartment to chase them away. Before he realized what was happening he was overwhelmed by a mob of Weatherpeople who left him, moments later, dazed and bleeding.

The police quickly collected themselves and the tide turned. By 10 o'clock, when the Weathermen began to scatter, police had arrested at least 70 members of the mob (30 or 40 of them Weatherman cadre). A number of Weathermen were badly beaten and three were shot: John Van Veenendaal, 22, of Seattle, through the neck, after he and another Weatherman allegedly attacked a policeman with clubs; Marshall Berzon, 22, of Hartford,

Connecticut; and Elizabeth Gardner, 26, of Seattle, the last two with buckshot. Much of the violence was the result of the Weatherman slogan, "Good revolutionaries don't get caught." Instead, they were to fight free. When the attempt failed, it was generally the worse for the arrestee.

That night the Weathermen regrouped at various movement centers, which included the Garett Theological Seminary and four Methodist churches, the Emmanuel, the Covenant United, the Wheadon and the Sherman, in Chicago and Evanston. Discussion centered on the obvious failure of the building actions since almost all those who had taken part had been cadre. Apparently they had recruited no one. An argument developed between those who felt the rest of the scheduled actions were politically necessary and should be undertaken as planned, regardless of numbers, and those who took the so-called "Tupamaros line" (a reference to the urban guerrilla movement in Uruguay) which argued that Weatherman should go underground immediately with the strength it retained and begin clandestine warfare against the United States. The Tupamaros line was defeated, at least for the moment, although a rock concert "wargasm" and a high-school raid were both canceled.

On Thursday morning, October 9, about 70 Weatherwomen marched to Grant Park for an all-women's action intended to end with a super-militant march on a Chicago draft board. Diana was one of the women taking part. When they arrived at the park wearing their boots, helmets and heavy jackets, they found themselves outnumbered by the police. During a rally they chanted "Oink

oink, bang bang, dead pig" and sang Weatherman songs
(some of which had been written by Ted Gold), including
one that borrowed an old civil-rights tune and went: "We
love our Uncle Ho Chi Minh, deep down in our hearts.
We love our Chairman Mao Tse-tung, deep down in our
hearts . . ." One of the speakers was Bernardine Dohrn,
who said Weatherwomen lived by the slogan, "Vietcong
women fight." Despite the odds, she said, they were going
to fight, too.

"This is not a self-indulgent bullshit women's movement," she said. "We refuse to be good Germans. We
live behind enemy lines."

At the end of the rally police stopped the women as
they tried to leave the park, insisting they would have to
drop their long poles and take off their helmets before
they would be allowed to proceed. A dozen women gritted
their teeth and charged into the ranks of police but were
immediately overpowered and arrested. The remainder,
some of them crying, allowed themselves to be disarmed
and escorted to the nearest subway station.

Later that day Diana was arrested by Chicago police
keeping an eye out for Weatherpeople wherever they
might turn up. On Friday Weatherman headquarters
called Diana's father in Dwight, told him his daughter
was being held in lieu of $500 bail and asked him to wire
the money so they could bail her out. Mr. Oughton said
he would take care of it himself and called an attorney he
knew. That evening the attorney drove Mr. Oughton to
Chicago, where he found that Diana's bail was not $500,
which would have demanded $50 in cash, but $5000, which

meant he had to find a place to cash a $500 check at eleven o'clock at night. It was nearly midnight by the time he paid the bail, then drove to another location where Diana was being held. When the police led her out she appeared subdued and tired. They got into the car and Mr. Oughton said, "I'm sure you need a rest. Why don't you come back to Dwight for a few days?"

"No," said Diana quickly, not wanting to argue the question. "I've got an important meeting in Evanston."

Shortly after 1:00 in the morning of Saturday, October 11, Mr. Oughton, the attorney and Diana pulled up in front of one of the Evanston churches. Diana said, "Good-by, Daddy," and hopped out. A small group of excited Weatherpeople crowded around her and she did not look back as her father and the attorney drove away.

Earlier that evening, while Mr. Oughton had been freeing his daughter, Weathermen from New York had discovered an undercover police agent in their headquarters at Emmanuel Methodist Church. The agent was beaten, of course, but finally released following the intervention of the minister of the church. Knowing that police would soon be arriving in strength, the Weathermen prepared to defend the church at all costs but then abandoned it on orders from the Weather Bureau. A couple of hours later, about 3:00 A.M. on Saturday, the Chicago and Evanston police, looking for those who had beaten the undercover agent, suddenly raided the church where most of the Weathermen were staying in Evanston. They arrested 43 Weathermen while the remainder, including Diana, escaped out the back door and by jumping out of the ground-floor windows.

The Weather Bureau, meanwhile, following another heated debate over strategy, had decided the march scheduled for Saturday should take place regardless of the danger involved. As soon as the action ended, Weatherpeople would be on their own. That afternoon Weathermen who had been keeping out of sight all day began arriving at the dynamited remains of the statue in Haymarket Square. The first group to arrive reached into shopping bags and pulled out helmets and denim jackets. Across the back of each jacket was the red and blue flag of the Vietcong and the legend, MOTOR CITY SDS. A few moments later police plainclothes men in the crowd of reporters and bystanders suddenly rushed the small group of Weatherleaders around the statue and dragged off four of them, including Jeff Jones, Mark Rudd (whom they recognized through a false beard) and Linda Evans. Despite this setback, John Jacobs gave a speech in which he said the Days of Rage had been a strategic victory even though clearly a tactical defeat. Fighting in the streets, he said, had been a necessary step. He did not say, but everyone knew, what the next step had to be.

When Jacobs finished the group moved off in a tightly knit mob, Motor City SDS in the front rank, breaking into a run as it left the park. No more than 200 Weathermen took part in the final rampage through the streets of Chicago. This time the police were better prepared and for each policeman bloodied in the fighting, 10 Weathermen were beaten senseless. By the end of the action, 103 Weatherpeople had been arrested and the rest were being hunted throughout the city.

That night Diana called a friend. She was elated by the

Days of Rage, but frightened as she tried to stay out of sight. She was accompanied by only one other Weatherman, a young man six inches shorter than herself, one of the men she had chosen to fill the gap left by Bill Ayers. "The pigs are picking everybody up," she told her friend over a pay phone. "Can you give me a ride to the airport? I've got to get back to Detroit." She did not mention the Weatherman with her.

The friend said no, she was sorry, and Diana hung up. Later that night she decided to head for Dwight, arriving early Sunday with her friend. As usual, Diana did not want to talk politics with her parents, but Mr. Oughton got into a familiar argument with the short Weatherman. He told Mr. Oughton he had been rejected by his family, the Army and every school he had ever attended; the only group which ever took him in, he said, had been SDS. Mr. Oughton found him irritatingly arrogant but remained courteous and polite. Diana's father was especially annoyed on Sunday when the short Weatherman beat him in the first four or five moves of a chess game.

Until Diana's arrest during the Days of Rage her family had no real idea who the Weathermen were or what they planned to do. Diana's mother was frightened and alarmed by the confused, incomplete account she received of the violent street fighting. In her loving but politically inarticulate way she tried to talk Diana into leaving the organization. "But, honey," she said, "you're only going to make things worse. You're only going to get yourself killed."

Diana did not want to argue the point. "It's the only way, Mummy," she said firmly. "It's the only way."

Going Underground

THE LEADERS OF WEATHERMAN insisted the Days of Rage had been a political victory, but in the following weeks it became apparent the victory was of a sort Weatherman would never have the strength to repeat. The organization took pride in the fact that it had forced Illinois's governor to call out the National Guard (although that was never used), in the number of police it had preoccupied, in the million dollars' worth of damage (by their estimate) caused during their two window-smashing forays. They argued that these represented "material damage" to imperialism and, therefore, concrete aid for the Vietnamese and other Third World revolutionaries.

Damage to imperialism, however, had been only half of Weatherman's purpose in holding the Days of Rage. More important had been their attempt to prove that confrontation could create a mass movement. This notion, bizarre in retrospect, was indisputably incorrect. Far from strengthening SDS, Weatherman, in just four months, had reduced it from the 2000 or so who had attended the June convention to the 400-odd street fighters, many of them only sixteen or seventeen years old, who broke windows in October. All the fighting over the summer and early fall had failed to recruit anyone; there was no disguising this brutal fact.

Weatherman's true assessment of the Days of Rage is better indicated by their actions than by their proclamations. After the national action the high-school raids and street fights came to an end. Weatherman continued to insist on its revolutionary ferocity, but behind that façade it was clearly an organization at the end of its tether.

Building for the Chicago action had strained Weatherman's resources to the limit. Legal difficulties alone threatened to swamp the organization. The law is notoriously slow, but it is also inexorable. By the end of October almost all of the arrested Weathermen were free on bail, but hundreds of them faced serious charges which would eventually come to trial. A partial list of those arrested for Weatherman actions between June and November includes nine at Macomb Community College, 26 during the Pittsburgh raid, 11 during a confrontation with police in a New York restaurant, 10 in the Detroit march, three in Flint, 290 during the Days of Rage and 23 in Boston in November for an alleged attack on a police station. The total of 372 arrests represented a huge amount of bail money as well as enormous organizational problems, since somebody or other was always due in court. While these

cases were pending the Weathermen were living on borrowed time: if they chose to fight the cases they would obviously have resources for nothing else; if they chose not
to fight, they would have to go into hiding.

During Weatherman's Indian Summer as a street-fighting organization it took part in two highly theatrical actions in Washington on the weekend of the great Mobiliza-
tion-Moratorium rally which drew hundreds of thousands
of people to the capital on November 15, 1969. On Thursday night, November 13, Bill Ayers and two other
Weathermen went to the headquarters of the Moratorium
(an organization of former McCarthy people particularly
detested by young revolutionaries) and, in effect, tried to
shake down the group for $20,000. In return for this token
of "fraternal solidarity," Ayers said, Weatherman would
make no attempt to turn Saturday's rally into a blood bath.
The demand was never presented in so many words, and
Sam Brown never acknowledged it by refusing it outright,
but those present had no doubt they were witnessing a
shakedown attempt. At one point during the vague but
threatening conversation Ayers was asked what the
Weatherman program was.

"Kill all the rich people," he answered. "Break up their
cars and apartments."

"But aren't your parents rich?" he was asked.

"Yeah," Ayers said. "Bring the revolution home, kill
your parents, that's where it's really at." *

---

* Accounts of this incident, from which these quotes are taken, have appeared in *Life*, November 28, 1969; the *Village Voice*, November 20,
1969; and the Washington *Post*, November 18, 1969.

On Friday night the Weathermen scuffled with police at Dupont Circle, near the South Vietnamese embassy, and on Saturday afternoon they did much the same outside the Department of Justice, immediately following the end of the vast rally at the Washington Monument. Compared to the Days of Rage, however, both actions were only high-spirited vandalism. They smashed windows, tossed back tear-gas cannisters and scampered about dodging police, but they made no effort to assault police or to fight free if they were captured. Fighting the police obviously brought more trouble than it was worth; Weathermen who had been beaten in Chicago were not eager to repeat the experience in Washington.

The Washington actions, for all their revolutionary melodrama, did not represent an attack on the state. Attorney General John Mitchell and the Weathermen were perfectly suited opponents, however, since both had a heavy vested interest in treating the sporadic violence as a matter for official alarm. Apparently in an attempt to scare away moderates, Mitchell had treated the rally as if it were a potential insurrection. When he said the day had been "violent" because of the Justice Department incidents, the Weathermen could hardly have been more flattered. Mitchell's wife later quoted him as comparing the excitement outside the Department with the Russian Revolution. Bill felt the same way. On the plane out of Washington the following day Ayers enthused to a friend, "You could see the red flags waving over this huge cloud of gas. It looked like the Russian Revolution. Outtasight!"

Following the Justice Department actions on Saturday,

Diana left her friends and crossed Washington to visit her younger sister Pam and meet, for the only time, Pam's husband. Carol was also there that night and Diana began telling her about the demonstration. She was excited by the drama of it and said she felt the revolution was near. Carol, equally interested in politics but far from being a revolutionary, was incredulous.

"When blue-collar workers are making six dollars an hour," she asked, "where is the support coming from?"

"The revolution is already taking place," Diana insisted. "It's a worldwide thing."

She was referring to Weatherman theory that the United States was only one battlefield in a worldwide class war. Revolutions did not take place in an international vacuum; the defeat of capitalism in the Third World would deprive the United States of essential raw materials and markets, starve the American economy and bring on a revolutionary crisis. For Diana and the Weathermen the revolution was not a matter of issues like wages and working conditions, "not just a dollar more" as Bill had said at Cleveland; it was an inevitable stage of world history. The revolution was coming whether American workers wanted it or not. The vision of the Weathermen was almost messianic in its intensity. Like Christians who can *see* the hand of God in history, leading inevitably to the Judgment, the Weathermen could see the unfolding of Marxian dialectic, leading inevitably to the revolution. The necessity of revolution is rooted in the natural order, they felt; it's as much a part of the way things are as the life and death of men, or of planets.

The faith in revolution had become a vital part of Diana's life, a tenet of belief which gave meaning to everything else. When Carol argued that conditions were not ripe for revolution, she might have been arguing that conditions were not ripe for the coming of spring; Diana felt both were equally inevitable.

In the fall of 1969 the Weathermen were willing to concede that few Americans agreed with their politics, just as evangelical Christians might concede that few Americans accept Christ as their savior. The fact that they stood alone, however, had nothing to do with the truth of their message. As evangelists are not lightly convinced there is no salvation, Diana was not easily convinced there would be no revolution.

Diana saw her parents and her sisters only once more. The day before Christmas she called to say she would be arriving later that night. Carol, who was also arriving Christmas Eve, arranged for a rented car to meet Diana at Chicago's O'Hare Airport. The family hoped she would arrive in time to help trim the tree but Diana did not enter the Oughton driveway on South Street until sometime after midnight. She was, as always, dressed in boots, blue jeans and a borrowed sweater and was carrying her toothbrush and nightie in a paper sack. On Christmas morning she was up early, talking happily to everyone in the family, going into the kitchen to kiss her old nanny, Ruth Moreheart, and to help make salad dressing. Diana chatted about Dwight for a moment, then asked Ruth, "What do you think of SDS?" Ruth was evasive and Diana turned cool.

During Christmas dinner at her uncle's house, Diana spent most of the time talking to her seventeen-year-old cousin, Jack, who was close to Diana in temperament and who was to be the last member of the family to see her. There was a degree of tension at the table since Jack's mother, China, was afraid Diana might be trying to recruit her son into the Weathermen. Diana was apologetic for not having brought any presents for the family but seemed genuinely pleased, for the first time in years, with the presents she was given: a heavy fisherman's sweater from Carol, a shirt and slacks from her mother.

During the previous few years Diana had generally been accompanied by friends whenever she came home. Mr. Oughton felt she needed the friends as protection against her family, as a kind of insurance that family feeling would not cool her revolutionary passions. The friends generally did most of the talking, raided the refrigerator with an arrogant air, were often rude to the family in an offhand way, and did all of those things to maintain a distance between Diana and her family which other revolutionaries, in their own homes, were generally eager to do for themselves. On Christmas, 1969, Diana's unprotected softness, her interest in the family and obvious pleasure at being with them, allowed Mr. Oughton to hope a change was coming, to believe that Diana was growing out of her passionate politics as she had every other condition of childhood, which, despite moments of doubt, he had always believed would happen.

After lunch the family pressed Diana to stay, but she insisted she had to leave. Their parting had an air of warmth, but no hint of finality. That afternoon she drove the rented car back to O'Hare Airport and then returned to Flint. Diana was not the only member of the Weathermen to go home for Christmas in 1969. The organization apparently hoped that sending its members home for the holiday would convince federal agents Weatherman was in the process of breaking up. The gesture confused a lot of families, but not the FBI.

Between December 27 and 31 Weatherman held its last open meeting, a well-publicized "war council" which attracted as much attention from the FBI and the Flint police as it did from the radical movement. The Weather Bureau had announced the council in a final issue of *New Left Notes,* published under the new name *Fire.* Included in the issue was a long criticism of Weatherman for various highly technical errors in ideology and practice, written by the Radical Education Project in Detroit, in which Jim Mellen was still active. The article was ridiculed by Howie Machtinger, elected to the NIC in June, 1969, and one of those mentioned as a co-conspirator in the federal bombing conspiracy indictment handed up in Detroit in July, 1970. Under the heading "Principles, shminciples," Machtinger rejected REP's argument with a simple reply: "Blah, blah, blah." No further analysis was considered necessary.

One of the reasons *New Left Notes–Fire* was killed was that words had ceased to carry any real meaning for Weathermen. They were interested only in action, and in the audience which could be gained by action. Mark Rudd, a self-admitted "creation of the media," held news conferences in Chicago on December 27 and in Flint the following day, when he spoke to reporters through a glass door which had been pierced by a rifle bullet. He was brusque: Weatherman would be deciding how to escalate the struggle in the 1970s.

About 400 people showed up for the council, including a number of underground reporters, radical sightseers and a contingent from Revolutionary Youth Movement II which hoped to salvage some remnant of SDS before the Weathermen succeeded in destroying it. The council was held in a large hall decorated with posters of movement heroes like Guevara, Castro and Ho Chi Minh. One wall was covered by alternating red and black portraits of Fred Hampton, leader of the Illinois chapter of the Black Panthers, who had been killed in his bed by Chicago police during a pre-dawn raid on December 4. On the second of the Days of Rage Hampton had spoken at an RYM II rally where he declared: "We oppose the anarchistic, adventuristic, chauvinistic, individualistic, masochistic and Custeristic Weathermen." Now he was a Weatherman martyr.

A large papier-mâché machine gun hung from the ceiling of the hall; a cardboard pistol rested on the floor near the door, where Weathermen frisked everyone entering the building. Signs proclaimed "Piece [that is, guns] now." The Weathermen talked of themselves as barbarians sent to destroy a decadent society, the twentieth-century equivalent of the Vandals and Visigoths who harried and finally destroyed the Roman Empire. They had stopped talking about politics; now they talked only of violence and savagery, of ripping, tearing, smashing, destroying.

At one point during the council Bernardine Dohrn cited Charles Manson and his family, alleged mass murderers, as examples of the savagery which Weathermen sought to emulate. "Dig it," she said, "first they killed those pigs, then they ate dinner in the same room with them, then they even shoved a fork into a victim's stomach. Wild!" For the rest of the council Weathermen greeted each other by holding up three fingers, symbol of the fork.

If the Weathermen had once considered themselves a "vanguard (which speaks) of important change to come," as Diana had written to her family only one year earlier, that time had passed; now the Weathermen were avenging angels. In their eyes the United States was guilty of moral crimes which placed all Americans outside the pale of humanity; no fate could be too severe. Weatherman saw no contradiction in making a revolution in the name of the people at the expense of the people. Like the Inquisitors of sixteenth-century Spain, they felt their larger purpose gave sanction to the cruelties of the moment.

During a heated argument about the relationship between the United States and the Third World in Weatherman theory, Ted Gold explained what would happen if the world revolution occurred elsewhere first. In that event, he said, the United States would be run "by an agency of the people of the world."

"In short," an opponent argued, "if the people of the world succeed in liberating themselves before the American radicals have made the American revolution, then the Vietnamese and Africans and the Chinese are going to move in and run things for white America. It sounds like a John Bircher's worst dream. There will have to be more repression than ever against white people, but by refusing to organize people, Weatherman isn't giving them half a chance."

"Well, if it will take fascism," Gold said, "we'll have to have fascism."

In another exchange Howie Machtinger attacked white workers for wanting to improve their living and working conditions while the rest of the world, most of it colored, lived in poverty and misery. They already benefited from their "white skin privilege," he said. Wanting even more made them racists.

Bob Avakian, a leader of RYM II, attacked him: "If you can't understand that white workers are being screwed, too, that they are oppressed by capitalism before they are racists, then that just shows your class origins."

Machtinger: "When you try to defend honky workers who just want more privilege from imperialism, that shows your race origins."

Weatherman's total commitment to the cause of black people struck most other radicals as suspiciously psychological rather than political in origin. Moralism ran through Weatherman theory like an infection: as whites, as Americans, as children of the upper classes they felt overprivileged. Their politics promised nothing to themselves, everything for others. Their selflessness was absolute. At the same time, however, they implicitly put themselves in a position to decide what was in the interests of the classes they wanted to help. They may have been "on a white guilt trip," as Bernardine Dohrn admitted during the council, but they still paid no attention to black criticism.

"All white babies are pigs," one Weatherman argued, meaning that whites oppress blacks from birth. When blacks disowned Weatherman's revolution, however, Weatherman simply paid no attention: they were fighting for blacks whether blacks wanted their aid, or not.

In her speech during the council Bernardine Dohrn conceded the Weathermen had been arrogant toward other movement people, but still insisted that white revolutionaries had to fight harder:

> We didn't fight around Bobby Seale when he was shackled at the conspiracy trial. We should have torn the courtroom apart. We didn't smash them when Mobe peace creeps hissed [Black Panther official] David Hilliard on Moratorium Day [November 15] in San Francisco. We didn't burn Chicago down when Fred [Hampton] was killed . . .
>
> Since October eleventh we've been wimpy on armed struggle . . . We're about being a fighting force alongside the blacks, but a lot of us are still honkies and we're still scared of fighting. We have to get into armed struggle.

This self-hate did not strike the rest of the radical movement as healthy or useful. Weathermen acted as if self-hate were the beginning of wisdom. They found in themselves a kind of original sin; loving themselves the less, they loved the revolution more. Mark Rudd expressed this peculiar selflessness at its most extreme. He told the council that Weatherman was "living the dialectic of life and death," that Weatherman's revolutionary exhilaration was the result of rooting out the bourgeois fear of violence. He called on white revolutionaries to live like Captain Ahab in *Moby Dick*, "with one thought: to bring down the white whale." The rest of the movement was only too keenly aware that it was Ahab, not the whale, who was destroyed in the end.

The Flint war council was a meeting of Weathermen talking to themselves; they were willing to allow a few former friends to listen, but they were not interested in arguing all the old questions over again. Those who came with doubts found most of them confirmed: Weatherman thinking had become heavy and crude; "democratic centralism" meant the Weather Bureau made all decisions; the celebration of random violence was attracting fifteen-year-old runaways, but no one else.

If the purpose of the council had been recruiting, it was a failure. Already doubtful about Weatherman's theory and emotional stability, the radical movement was completely alienated by Weatherman's emphasis on *any* kind of violence, directed at *any* target, under *any* circumstances. The raptures of the converted are easily dismissed by the skeptical. Weathermen tried to convince by the intensity of their own revolutionary fervor; to the unconvinced, they simply appeared unbalanced.

The failure of the council and the legal problems pressing in on the Weathermen made it obvious the organization could not go on as it had. During the Days of Rage a dispute had flared between those who supported mass actions in the street and holders of the Tupamaros line urging clandestine warfare. By the end of December, Weatherman was ready to embrace the latter. During the council a dozen Weatherman leaders met secretly on the other side of Flint in the Sacred Heart Catholic Church, where they decided Weatherman must purge every doubtful member and go underground. According to Flint Police Chief James Rutherford, Diana and Cathy Wilkerson were both at the secret meeting.

During the council the Weathermen also concluded that the attempt to "smash monogamy" had been a failure. Making plans to go underground in small groups, they decided that close personal relationships would be a source of strength, both practically and emotionally. Bill and Diana had several long conversations at Flint and later, during which they decided that perhaps it was permissible for them to love each other after all. When the council ended, however, they separated again, Bill having business in Chicago and Diana involved with collectives in Detroit and Ann Arbor. They felt they were making a new beginning. Time, however, was short, and the new beginning led to nothing.

After the council ended on New Year's Eve the leaders of Weatherman returned to Chicago. *New Left Notes* and the print shop which had produced it were already gone. Early in the new year, the Weathermen completed what they had begun the previous June. They systematically destroyed everything in the SDS headquarters at 1608 West Madison Street, burning pamphlets, reports, position papers, leaflets, resolutions, correspondence, contact files, financial records, back issues of *New Left Notes* and the minutes of eight years of conventions, National Councils and meetings of the National Interim Committees.

By 1970 SDS was little more than the paper which recorded its history; the Weathermen destroyed the history, too. There was little among these papers that referred to Weatherman, or that could have been used to any advantage by police. The Weathermen destroyed the records of SDS for two reasons: first, to prevent its renaissance after they went underground. They intended that white radicals would do it their way, or not at all. Second, they were in the mood to indulge a final gesture of contempt for all who were not with them. When they left the office, the white student-movement which SDS had once led was dead.

During the two months between the destruction of the old SDS office and the explosion on March 6, the Weathermen attempted to create an underground organization of urban guerrillas which would escalate the war against America. Of the 400 radicals who attended the Flint war council, fewer than 100 were chosen, or allowed, to join the Weathermen underground. The rest either decided things had gone far enough, or were purged on suspicion of being police spies or political weaklings. The old Weather Bureau recreated itself as a central organizing committee which would communicate with a network of small Weatherman collectives, modeled after the "affinity group" created by the Motherfuckers 18 months earlier, through telephone answering services and anonymous post office boxes.

The Weatherman collectives, ranging in size from 10 to 30 or more, broke up into four- and five-man groups and moved out of their old quarters. Weathermen cut, and sometimes dyed, their hair, dropped their most flamboyant habits and began keeping a constant eye out for the police. All the usual paraphernalia of radicals — posters, leaflets, buttons — disappeared. In their place the Weathermen assembled arsenals.

On February 2 Diana called to wish Carol a happy birthday in Washington. Diana had always felt close to Carol. Over the years she told Carol far more about her life with Bill and her work with SDS than she ever mentioned to any other member of the family. She also told Carol things about herself, about her desire for a child and the year during which she and Bill tried to have one, about her mixed feelings about her childhood. Diana's warmth during the phone call again suggested to Carol that perhaps she was on the verge of splitting from the Weathermen.

On February 4 Diana flew to Chicago for a court appearance stemming from her arrest during the Days of Rage. At first the Weathermen had made a practice of demanding jury trials in order to clog Chicago court calendars and thereby further impair the smooth operation of imperialism. By the time Diana appeared in February, however, the organization had moved on to more pressing matters and Diana pleaded guilty. She was fined $450 which, with legal costs, equalled the $500 bail put up by her father. When her name was called out the judge looked up and asked, "Are you related to Jim Oughton, the legislator?"

With a smile of amusement, Diana admitted that she was.

After leaving the court, she visited her cousin Jack at Northwestern, and he became the last member of the family to see her. Later that day she called her old friend Karin Rosenberg and was invited for dinner. She knew Karin lived on the edge of Chicago's South Side ghetto and asked, "Is it safe?"

"Of course," Karin said. "Why do you ask?"

"You don't know how deep the hate of the black man is," Diana answered.

When she arrived she was wearing her usual suede boots, blue jeans and woolen man's shirt. Karin had grown accustomed to seeing Diana thin and weary, but this time she was drawn to the point of illness, her eyes dark and deep, her cheekbones painfully high, her long fingers almost skeletal, her hair a dead, dirty blond. Diana looked not just tired, but on the edge of exhaustion; not just underfed, but starved.

The evening was an awkward one. Political differences had long since made Karin's husband slightly uneasy around Diana, and the conversation often lagged. Diana was vague about what she was doing. In the past she had always answered that question by saying "high-school organizing," but now she did not even mention that. She talked about Cuba for a while, praising the political sophistication of Cuban workers. The Weathermen and the Vietnamese, she said, "understood each other." She doubted, with a smile, that Karin and Merrill would like Cuba, or be welcome there. At another point, she casually referred to the Chicago 7 as "fascist pigs" for having allowed their trial to proceed after the severance of the eighth defendant, Bobby Seale. She mentioned that the 16 people in her collective had decided to break up into four- and five-man groups to avoid harassment by the police.

The Rosenbergs had tickets for the ballet so the evening ended early. They dropped Diana off in the Loop and said good-by. Diana kissed Karin, which she had not done for a long time, and made sure Karin had the new SDS address in Detroit, a box number since the group was moving from place to place. A few days later Diana sent Karin a reprint of the Weatherman manifesto as it had appeared in the June *New Left Notes*. Across the top was a brief message: "Karin — I'd love to talk to you about this — Love, Diana."

Before returning to Detroit that night Diana called home to tell her parents her fine had used up all her father's bail money. "You know, Diana," her mother said, "you're killing us both."

"I'm sorry, Mummy," Diana answered.

At about the same time that month, Diana went to see an old friend in Ann Arbor, Lidie Howes, the mother of one of the children at the Community School, to ask if SDS could use Mrs. Howes's basement for occasional meetings. It was the first time she had seen Mrs. Howes in months and they talked for hours, sitting over coffee in the kitchen, about politics, the Days of Rage, and Diana's trip to Cuba. Mrs. Howes said the Chicago actions had struck her as simple hoodlumism which would only alienate potential allies. Diana admitted it might, but insisted it was a necessary step toward revolution. "People have to learn to confront violence," she said.

Mrs. Howes asked if she meant the Weathermen were trying to bring violence home to the American people, to make them realize what was happening to the Vietnamese.

"No, it's not that at all," Diana said. "People simply have to learn to confront violence."

Diana told Mrs. Howes about the Cuba trip, mentioning the progress made in health care and education. Privileges had been ended, she said, and factory workers, even at the lowest level, took part in making the decisions which affected their lives. "Isn't it much better for people to work for the good of everybody instead of just for themselves?" she asked.

Mrs. Howes doubted that Cuban workers really made the important decisions and wondered why there was so little political freedom there. She asked how Diana felt about the hundreds of executions which had followed Castro's rise to power. Diana seemed never to have heard of them. Mrs. Howes asked about freedom of the press and about the system of neighborhood spies who reported to the police on political dissidents.

Diana didn't think the spying caused much harm. "If you're for the revolution you have nothing to fear," she said. When Mrs. Howes tried to press her about the lack of basic freedoms, Diana dismissed the objection. "I'm not a civil liberties person," she said.

At the end of the afternoon Diana got up to go. "I came to ask if the local SDS could meet in your basement," she said, "but now I don't know what you think of us any more." She was not angry, Mrs. Howes felt, just disappointed.

Mrs. Howes was not the only person Diana approached on behalf of Weatherman during these weeks. She also proposed a "simple rip-off" to a friend who had never heard of the term. Diana asked the friend to buy some traveler's checks, give them to Diana and report them lost. Diana would cash them and the friend would be reimbursed by the company. The friend turned her down but felt bad about doing so, since Diana seemed in such need of the money. Other Weathermen proposed similar schemes to friends, or simply asked to borrow money that clearly would never be paid back.

The Weathermen had decided that among their principal assets were friends and family; during the Days of Rage they had counted on parents, for example, to provide most of the bail money. Early in 1970 the Weathermen also may have been selling hard drugs as a means of raising funds; Diana, at any rate, was seen carrying glassine envelopes of cocaine or heroin (the observer was not sure which), and she is not known to have ever tried either drug.

On Monday, March 2, Diana called her sister Carol in Washington. The two girls had a long conversation, mostly about the family. Diana asked if Debbie was still a Republican and if Carol had a boyfriend. She asked about their parents and mutual friends and life in Dwight. A certain tone of emotional need, something more urgent than simple nostalgia, touched Diana's questions and

Carol, again, allowed herself to hope that Diana was having doubts about the Weathermen.

Halfway through the conversation Diana abruptly asked, "Will the family stand by me, no matter what? Will they help me if I need it?"

"Of course," Carol said. "Anything."

Later Diana asked if she could send Carol some personal papers. "The pigs have been rifling through our house," she said. "They [the papers] aren't anything important but I just don't want anybody to find them."

A couple of days later a large envelope arrived marked N'OUVREZ PAS (Do not open). Diana had not used French expressions in her letters for years; Carol supposed that someone else must have written it there. Nevertheless, she did not open the envelope until after Diana's death. Inside were letters from old friends, including the priests she had known in Guatemala; an address book; pages from a 1969 appointment book; documents about the family farm corporation; scraps of paper with names and addresses: everything, in short, which conceivably could have been used by police to identify her.

Carol still feels that Diana was reconsidering her commitment to revolution, that the intensity of her interest in the family betrayed an emotional hunger for escape from the violently political atmosphere of the Weathermen. Even if that was so, however, Diana gave no other indication that she was not fully determined to go ahead with the plans for terrorism which she had helped to formulate. Diana's undeniable love for her family was one of the things which had always made other white revolutionaries doubt her commitment; for that reason she came home seldom, and then usually with a protective screen of friends.

The mother of one of the children at the Children's Community School had watched Diana showing her father around the school in the fall of 1967. She was startled to hear Diana call him "Daddy" and to sense how desperately Diana wanted to impress him. The school was everything to Diana at that time; she wanted her father to see what an extraordinary experiment it was. The school, like everything else they discussed during that period, simply became a subject for argument. When it became clear that argument would never lead to agreement, Diana simply abandoned the subject of politics at home. The alternative would have been increasing acrimony and a final break. For as long as it was possible, she tried to balance the two, politics and family, without abandoning either. A sign of her strength was that in the end she did not allow her love for her family to prevent her from doing what she was convinced had to be done.

With the exception of Diana's continuing love for her family, her situation within Weatherman was not unique. It was no accident that Weatherman had a reputation as a pack of spoiled children of the rich; they were overwhelmingly from America's privileged classes. The majority of the radical movement, for example, felt the quality of life in Weatherman collectives did not reflect a victory over bourgeois hangups about cleanliness, but the casual contempt for order of children who have always been picked-up-after by maids. No one except the rich, said Weatherman's critics, would ever have supposed that the poor *liked* violence.

The Weathermen themselves joked that the first test for membership was a father who made at least $30,000 a year. In fact, Weatherman tended to attract movement radicals who were the most sensitive to the charge their commitment was shallow. Black militants had often attacked whites for playing at revolution, since their white skins guaranteed them a place in society while blacks had everything to lose. Of all the white radical organizations, SDS was always the most sensitive to this charge, and the most eager to disprove it by militance.

Weatherman began as an SDS faction which attracted all those who could most easily return to the establishment whenever the going got rough. It was not only black militants, but their parents, their teachers, and their friends who suggested white radicals were only summertime soldiers. Even the police and the courts seemed to share the belief. White radicals got hit over the head from time to time and were occasionally sentenced to thirty days in jail for disturbing the peace, while Black Panthers like Fred Hampton were killed. There was only one way white radicals could defend themselves against this charge: to become criminals, for whom there would be no longer any choice of returning to straight society.

In turning against society, however, the Weathermen were also turning against themselves, since it was their world which they considered to be the enemy. It was their country that was holding back the world revolution; it was their class which ruled the country; it was their own families who had raised them to take a place in the ruling class. The Weathermen felt they contained within themselves the seed of everything they opposed. Inside the organization, they turned savagely on each other and on themselves in an attempt to root out that seed. In Dwight, Diana had hated being rich; in Guatemala, she had hated being an American; in the Weathermen she finally came to hate herself. How else could she have tried so desperately to destroy everything that she was?

At Bryn Mawr and in Guatemala, Diana had begun by trying to help people in limited but concrete ways. By early 1970 she was preparing to dedicate herself to terrorism. Like most other Weathermen, she secretly wondered if these extremes could be truly reconciled. It was not a doubt which could be shared, however. Weathermen did not question the necessity of smashing the old regime; the commitment to terrorism had been made by the group. She could either stand by her friends, as she and they had sworn they would again and again and again over the years, or she could abandon them. There was no middle ground.

Faced by a similar choice at every step of the gradual transformation of SDS into the Weathermen, hundreds of others had decided to drop out. Diana was one of the last hundred, who placed loyalty above everything else. When the Weathermen became everything she had hated in the beginning — dogmatic, anti-democratic, violent and cruel — Diana still remained with her friends. It was not so much a question of ideology, as a question of honor.

Diana had called Carol from Detroit on Monday, March

2. On the same day, in Keene, New Hampshire, a Weatherman purchased (for under $60) two 50-pound cases of dynamite from the New England Explosives Corporation. Sometime that week the dynamite, or at least part of it, was driven from Keene to New York where it was carried into the house at 18 West Eleventh Street. That week, also, Diana left Detroit for New York and joined the small group staying in the house while Cathy Wilkerson's father was in the Caribbean.

In the middle of the week, probably on Wednesday, Diana met Alan Howard. They talked about politics and, inevitably, the Weathermen. Diana admitted the Days of Rage had been a limited success, at best; that the Flint war council had achieved nothing useful; that revolution was impossible without a mass base of support. Nevertheless, she said, building a Red Army was a necessary step and her role, personally, was to be one of its soldiers. "We have a lot to learn," she said. "We'll make mistakes."

Sometime on Friday morning Diana and a young man (later identified by the Weathermen as Terry Robbins) went down into the basement at 18 West Eleventh Street, where Cathy Wilkerson's father had built a workbench in an area he used for refinishing antiques. Using clocks, wire, batteries, detonating caps and dynamite, Diana and the young man began putting together bombs. A few minutes before noon, one of them attached a wire in the wrong place.

Home to Dwight

On TUESDAY, March 24, 1970, Diana was buried in the Oughton family plot, next to her grandparents on a faint rise, in the cemetery a mile and a half west of Dwight. It was a clear, crisp, sunny day. The family was there, along with members of Dwight's two other leading families and a few of Diana's old friends from Dwight days, from Bryn Mawr and from Guatemala. Mrs. Oughton spoke briefly with one of Diana's Bryn Mawr friends, wondering if things might have worked out better if only Diana had married John Henrich. The friend did not know what to respond. The emotional shock felt by those at the funeral was shared by others who had known Diana.

In New York, the day after Diana had been identified, John and Nancy Frappier and their two children visited the site of the explosion and left some flowers and the CHILDREN ARE ONLY NEWER PEOPLE button which Diana had designed. Letters about Diana started to arrive at the Oughton home a day or two later. Mr. Oughton expected to hear from Bill Ayers; he had once considered Bill his friend, but Bill did not write, then or later. The family heard from only one of Diana's friends in SDS, a girl who had lived with her in a Detroit collective and who had been arrested during the Pittsburgh raid in September, 1969.

> Our faction of SDS was excessive in its attempts to stifle and kill certain tendencies [she wrote]. Nevertheless, Diana was always sensitive to human feelings and needs . . . Weatherman lost many people who wanted to retain that sensitivity. It became an organization of those who were either cold in the first place or who had found a way to conceal their gentility. Unfortunately, repression is the method of killing a characteristic. Diana managed to hang on to her beautiful sensitivity for an incredibly long time.

Dozens of other friends who had lost track of Diana after Madeira or Bryn Mawr or the closing of the Children's Community School read of her death and tried, and failed to reconcile the Diana they had known with the woman who died in the basement of a New York townhouse.

In Dwight itself there was a brief flurry of excitement as reporters and television crews invaded the town looking for an explanation of Diana's death. What they learned only deepened the mystery: her life had once promised so much, and was sacrificed for so little. The citizens of Dwight were as uncomprehending as people elsewhere. They had seen little of Diana since the fall of 1956, when she had gone away to school. They remembered her as a blond little girl, or not at all. When *Time* magazine ran a full-page story on Diana not long after her identification, the three copies delivered every week to Dwight's only newsstand were purchased in minutes. The Diana in *Time*'s story was no one they had known.

One of the few townspeople aware of the Oughtons' long anxiety over their daughter told Patrick Cleary, editor of the Dwight *Star and Herald*, at the time of the funeral, "It must be a relief, in a way. At least now they know where their daughter is." Cleary, a longtime friend of Mr. Oughton who had lived in Dwight all his life, later tried to explain the town's dim comprehension of what had happened: "Most of the people here in Dwight thought she was just a hippie — you know, long hair, anti-soap, love everybody. They didn't know she was in a movement like the Weathermen. I knew it, but it was just one of those unfortunate things. You didn't go up and down the street telling people about it."

As early as September, 1969, when Diana had called to say she would not be coming to Pam's wedding, Mrs. Oughton had sensed she was going to lose her daughter. She began to build a kind of wall in her mind to strengthen herself for the break. Mr. Oughton, a man of questioning temperament, brooded over the death of his daughter, trying to understand what had happened. Shortly after she had been identified he told one reporter that Diana had been the victim of a kind of "intellectual hysteria," of a feverish reasoning which, while remaining internally consistent, perhaps, had lost contact with reality.

When Kathy Boudin and Cathy Wilkerson failed to appear in court in Chicago on Monday, March 16, it was clear the Weathermen were determined to continue despite the disaster on West Eleventh Street. On March 30 another ten Weathermen failed to appear in a Chicago court. The following day a Chicago apartment allegedly rented by Weathermen was searched by police who found weapons, ammunition and 59 sticks of dynamite. On April 2 a federal grand jury in Chicago indicted twelve Weathermen leaders, including Bill Ayers, on charges of violating the federal anti-riot statute in planning the Days of Rage. Diana was one of those named, but not indicted, as co-conspirators. On April 15 the FBI in New York arrested three Weathermen on various charges; all were later to be charged in the bombing conspiracy indictment handed up by a Detroit federal grand jury on July 23. Bill Ayers was again one of those charged, and Diana one of those named as a co-conspirator. Three other Weathermen were also arrested in connection with the second indictment but the rest escaped.

The result of the explosion on West Eleventh Street, and of the indictments which followed it, was the complete disappearance of all the Weathermen who remained free, probably at a date much earlier than they had planned. They continued to set off bombs at periodic intervals and in September they helped free Timothy Leary from a minimum-security prison in San Luis Obispo, California, where he was serving a long term for possession of marijuana. Before leaving the United States for Algeria, Leary spent two weeks in hiding with Bill Ayers and Bernardine Dohrn. He told friends later they had seemed far more subdued than he had once imagined them.

People who had known Bill and Diana in Ann Arbor half expected the third body would turn out to be his. Unaware of what had been happening inside Weatherman, they found it hard to imagine Diana involved in bombing if he were not involved, too. In fact, Bill was in Michigan when the bomb exploded and his reaction, after learning that Diana was one of the dead, was said to have been "stoic." On April 10 he visited some old friends in New York (who later moved to the country, sick of politics and cities) and that summer he was seen in Ann Arbor from time to time. After the bombing conspiracy indictment was handed up in July, Ayers, along with the rest of the Weathermen, disappeared completely.

The Weathermen never contacted the families of Diana or Ted Gold or Terry Robbins, but they quickly began to exploit all three as martyrs in the war against American imperialism. In a statement released in Chicago by Bernardine Dohrn in May, the Weathermen promised the war had begun, not ended.

> For Diana Oughton, Ted Gold and Terry Robbins, and for all the revolutionaries who are still on the move here, there has been no question for a long time now — we will never go back.

Terry's father refused to believe his son was dead, however, and the third body from the house on West Eleventh Street was never claimed from the morgue of New York's chief medical examiner.

Underground papers ran obituaries about Diana and Ted Gold, vague on the facts of their lives but confident of their political significance. The question of terrorism was avoided, although some writers argued that the dynamite bomb which killed them was a pitifully minor instance of violence compared to the devastation caused by a single B-52 raid in Vietnam.

At first the underground press was drawn to the Weathermen by the romance of their daring, but after a bomb killed a young man in a mathematics research center at the University of Wisconsin in August, some of the enchantment began to wear off. Radicals continued to think of bombing as a symbolic gesture, a way of pointing out the enemy, but it began to be apparent that, so far, bombing had achieved nothing, and that all it might ever be expected to achieve would be a larger FBI, tougher laws and an assault on the underground press.

The Weathermen, in constant fear of police and finding it difficult to maintain contact with each other, continued to release occasional statements and claimed credit for a series of bombings in the fall of 1970. Some of the Weathermen moved to California, some were said to have spent the summer in rural New Mexico, and three were reported to have fled to Cuba. At least one Weatherman decided the cause was hopeless and, away from the heated political meetings which had once allowed Weatherman's enthusiasms to seem plausible, he retired to a farm in New England. Others, too, were said to be losing heart.

Despite arrests and defections, however, Weatherman could be expected to survive. There was still much they had not done: they had not tried kidnaping, nor had they deliberately killed anyone. They might still be criticized from their left, for holding back, for not being *really* committed, for being "wimpy about armed struggle," for retaining bourgeois hangups about murder. More important, Weatherman had become an institution, and institutions have a tenacious grip on life once they exist. Most tenacious of all are those institutions which serve a faith beyond argument.

Critics of the Weathermen had often compared them to the equally elite Narodniki in Russia, a terrorist group which set back the cause of reform by decades when they assassinated Czar Alexander in 1881. The Narodniki, always a small organization, assassinated Russian officials over a fifty-year period despite the fact it was sometimes reduced to only three or four active members, and was actually headed during one ten-year period by an agent for the Czarist secret police.

Other examples of the tenacity of institutions exist closer to home: the United States contains dozens of sects which have splintered off from the major Protestant churches, tiny groups, sometimes no more than a few dozen in number, who have kept their eccentric faiths alive for decades, sometimes even centuries, despite prejudice, official harassment and the scorn of skeptics. Being strong, they do not flinch merely because they stand alone. Diana's human warmth made her loved in Weatherman; many of her friends wept when they learned she had died. It is not hard to imagine there will continue to be Weathermen loyal to her memory, who will go on bombing in her name.

Appendices

Appendix 1

At the Weatherman conference held in Cleveland August 29–September 1, 1969, Bill Ayers gave a long speech which captured Weatherman's thinking and style at a moment when the organization still felt revolution was coming to the United States in the immediate future. The text which follows was published in the September 12, 1969, issue of New Left Notes. *The confidence which infuses Ayers's speech contrasts sharply with the Weatherman statement in Appendix III, released only fifteen months later.*

LAST WEEK I went up to St. Johns in New Brunswick with a couple of other people to meet with the people who had come back from Cuba and a meeting with the PRG. The reason we went up there is because we felt they had been out of the country six weeks, that a lot of contradictions had been heightened, especially between us and RYM II, that a lot of changes had taken place all over this country, and we felt that the people might be totally out of it and should be cued in to what was going on.

The first thing that I found out when I got up there was that there wasn't a whole lot of straightening out that needed to be done, because in fact a lot of changes we had gone through here they had gone through also. They had been involved in the process of building cadre just as we had, they had had some confrontations with a few members of the running dogs (RYM II) who were down there, so it wasn't a terrible problem the way we had anticipated it would be.

One of the things I did while I was there was that I talked a lot about the criticisms that have been made of the national action. I talked particularly about the charge that we are adventurist which people hear a lot, that somehow the national office, and Weatherman in particular and the Weather Bureau in specific, are a bunch of adventurist fools who are out to get us all killed. I talked about that, and one of the things I said is that adventurism is when you don't believe that you can organize the people, and lose confidence in the people, and therefore totally cut yourself off from everything, and you develop a strategy for losing, which of course is not what we're involved in at all. I also talked about the fact that if it is a worldwide struggle, if Weatherman is correct in that basic thing, that the basic struggle in the world today is the struggle of the oppressed peoples against U.S. imperialism, then it is the case that nothing we could do in the mother country could be adventurist. Nothing we could do because there is a war going on already, and the terms of that war are set. We couldn't be adventurist while there is genocide going on in Vietnam and in the black community.

Later on in the conversation, people criticized me for that statement, and they said it was wrong to say that genocide is being committed in Vietnam, because that communicated a number of non-struggle things — that the Vietnamese are sad, tired old people who are persecuted by the evil United States. In fact that's not what the Vietnamese are about. The Vietnamese are strong, the most heroic and the most incredible people in the world, and they've beaten U.S. imperialism — they've defeated the United States. That lesson is very important for us because it teaches us that struggle against U.S. imperialism is possible, that when we fight U.S. imperialism we have a chance of winning, that even a small nation, relatively unarmed, can hold off 500,000 U.S. troops, can defeat them in every way — that the Vietnamese have won, that they are strong, that the United States is not indestructible, not some kind of monolith that can never be changed, that history is not static, that the people can win.

Bernadette Devlin, when she was here last week, said a similar thing: that our greatest weakness is our belief in our weakness, and that's certainly true in the mother country here. What we have to communicate to people is our strength, and to show people our strength we have to show them the strength of fighting on the side of the worldwide movement. So I was criticized for projecting the image of weakness. It's a similar thing if people have seen this Wilmington, Delaware thing that Newsreel did. The kind of image that that creates about black people is that they're downtrodden, that DuPont is this heavy thing that is screwing these black people, as if they're so beaten down that they can't move. The film is essentially useless, because it conveys that kind of notion, that imperialism has defeated the people, whereas the Huey Newton film and the first Panther film conveys just the opposite: it conveys strength, it conveys confidence, it conveys positiveness, it conveys all those kinds of things that we have to learn to convey to people, all those kinds of things in terms of the image that the Vietnamese have tried to project to the world. It's no longer that we can make posters about Vietnam with an old man and a little kid who are burned by napalm. The posters that we put out and the truth is the symbol of a woman with a gun, or the picture of Nguyen Van Troi, the hero who was captured and later shot for attempting to assassinate McNamara in 1964. And Van Troi, handcuffed to the post where he was to be shot and screaming at his assassins, screaming "Long live people's war! Death to U.S. imperialism!" That's the image of Vietnam, it's that strength, that confidence and that's what we have to bring to our own constituency, it's that that we have to integrate into our politics in a positive way. That's one of the major things that we have to deal with in terms of the national action. We have to deal with the fact that in a lot of ways all of us have elements of defeatism in us, and don't really believe that we can win, don't really believe that the United States can be beaten. But we have to believe it, because defeatism is based on individualism — it is really based on the thought that I can't beat U.S. imperialism, I'm going to die, I'm going to get wiped out. But the Vietnamese people have won, and that fact makes it a lie to say that we can't win or that we won't win. We have won, we won in Vietnam, that was a victory for us and for all people, and we will continue to win, continue to defeat U.S. imperialism. We have to stamp out that individualist notion that if I don't make it through the next year, if I don't make it to construct socialism within twenty years, that that is a defeat. That's a defeatist and individualist attitude and we have to beat that attitude out of ourselves.

One of the things about the politics of confidence and the politics of victory is that we know if we have good politics, if we stick closely to Weatherman, if we project that analysis of worldwide struggle and our part in that, that we have essentially the answers to the questions that people are asking for. We have answers for people that other politics don't have. For instance, when people in Detroit go into a drive-in, and talk to those kids about the war and about the international struggle, and talk to those people about racism, and male supremacy and pigs, they're not just talking on an intellectual level and saying see, here's what's happening, this is why you're fucked up, because these kids know that already. We don't have to say to people what's wrong, we have to say to people what do you do about it. And that concretely is what actions in Detroit, in Chicago, in Ohio and other places have communicated. We can't project that phony kind of image that you join the movement because you get a dollar more an hour, you join it because you get *New Left Notes,* some bullshit — though that's a good thing, not a bad thing. You join the movement because you want to be part of that worldwide struggle that's obviously winning, and you win people over to it, and you win people over by being honest to them about the risks, by being honest to them about the struggle, by being honest to them that what they are getting into is a fight: it's not a comfortable life, it's not just a dollar more, it's standing up in the face of the enemy, and risking your life and risking everything for that struggle. But it's also being on the side of victory, and that's the essential thing that we have to show people.

In terms of building for the national action, this is what we have to project. We have to build this confidence, and build this power, we have to feel this power, and that's why it was so important to start this weekend off by talking about the Vietnamese, by talking about that power, by talking about that worldwide struggle. At this point I think it is also important to talk about the historical period that we're in, the importance of our job. A lot of people tend to ignore the role we have to play and therefore allow themselves all kinds of luxuries of being sloppy in their work and not pushing people, and being liberal toward other people because they don't understand the necessity of what we're doing right now, including the total importance of this fall for our politics. I think that the national action has to be seen in the context of a strategy that's going to win, that's going to support the NLF concretely, that's going to build Weatherman, and that's going to build a fighting revolutionary youth movement. We can't get involved anymore in the kinds of actions that merely say to people that this is wrong, or that is wrong, because that doesn't tell people what to do, that doesn't project the kind of confidence, and the crucial nature and importance of what we're trying to do in this country now. We have to fight and show people through struggle our commitment, our willingness to run risks, our willingness to die in the struggle to defeat U.S. imperialism. We have to convey these things, and October 8–11 is a concrete way that we can do that. I think people should push out this slogan "Bring the war home." We're not just saying bring the troops home and deploy them some other place, we're saying bring the war home. We're saying you're going to pay a price because increasingly guys in the army are going to shoot you in the back, increasingly the guys in the army are going to shoot over the heads of the Vietnamese, shoot over the heads of the blacks, increasingly this country is going to be torn down, and we're not going to bring the troops home to be deployed someplace else, we're going to bring the war home, we're going to create class war in the streets and institutions of this country, and we're going to make them pay a price, and the price ultimately is going to be total defeat for them. That's the kind of thing that we have to convey, and that's the kind of thing that we have to build.

I think people understand how this kind of action at this time, given the whole thing in Paris and the situation the Vietnamese are in now, can concretely aid the Vietnamese.

The other thing that people have to get confident about is that we can build a revolutionary youth movement. There's a lot of skepticism in some places about whether this action can come off, and that skepticism comes out of one thing, and that is that people have been listening to so-called "movement people," and these "movement people" have been telling them that it won't work, that it's adventurist, that it's going to hurt people, and that it's not right at this time, that we have to build a united front, or some other bullshit. And these movement people, this kind of right wing force, this weirdness that's moving around, it's all these old people who came into the movement at a time when pacifism was important, at a time when there was a total consciousness of defeat, when the only reasons that we were in it were moral reasons, when there was no strategy for victory, for gaining power, so that the people who came into the movement at that time have a certain kind of consciousness and belief about what is possible, and what we have to do is not listen to the *Guardian*, or what the *Guardian* thinks is possible, not to listen to other "movement" groups, like certain local Newsreels, certain local NOCs, and think they must know what's right because they are "the movement." If you think you've been isolated sometimes in your local work, you've got to dig what happened in Detroit, where because of the actions that people were taking, every so-called "movement group" in the city started to get together in a coalition to stop SDS. When the MC 9 were arrested and put in prison, and Motor City SDS people tried to raise money, they had responses from some of these so-called movement people that it would be better to leave them in jail, because they'd be dangerous on the streets. But the point is that to judge our actions by what those fucking people have to say about them is crazy. We have to go to the people and see what they have to say about the actions. Anybody who has been out to a high school or to a drive-in, to a community college in an aggressive and assertive way knows that the people out there loved the fuckin' action, and thought that it was out of sight.

We have to understand that if we're going to build our movement, if our movement is going to go forward and develop a different class basis and fight privilege, and fight on the side of the Vietnamese and the blacks, that a lot of these so-called movement people are just going to have to get out of the way, drop out, and that's what should happen to them — that's what their class interest is. But we don't have to listen to what they have to say and get defeatist, we have to get out to more and more people. It's not so much that these people as individuals, as people, have to be smashed or destroyed or anything like that, it's that those ideas, those tendencies, those notions have to be totally discredited, smashed and destroyed. And in the process of doing that, some of those individuals will come over. They won't understand if we sit and talk about it, they'll only understand if we smash their ideas.

In places where we smashed ideas and built our movement off of toughness and combated liberalism in ourselves, we've developed the best struggles in this country. It happened at Columbia, it happened in Michigan-Ohio.

The whole region in Michigan-Ohio was built by destroying the right wing in a couple of chapters, and asserting the power to throw them out of the chapters. But in order for us to really accomplish this, in order for us to really gain in this kind of struggle, a lot of the business that we have to be about is transforming ourselves, by getting rid of the things that are slowing us down and holding us back. This means that the only way we're going to gain that confidence and build that fighting movement, and to get rid of those bourgeois things in ourselves, is by developing collectives off struggle, and off outreach, and to build them off internal struggle — but the internal struggle only makes sense when there's outreach going on.

A lot of the problems that people are going through now have to do with monogamy and its basis in male supremacy. What we have to understand in this whole discussion is that we have one task, and that's to make ourselves into tools of the revolution. We know what we have to do and that means a lot of heavy stuff. It means a lot of invading things that people didn't think should be invaded before, and it means a lot of resisting. Just this morning a guy was saying to me that I know that what I'm saying about monogamy has to do with my own bourgeois hang-ups, but my bourgeois hang-ups are more important to me than being a communist at this point. That's something that just had to be smashed. The reason that this thing comes up at all is not just about people liking to be house-wreckers or some shit, it's got to do with the fact that people have come to see the need to build collectives that are strong and tough, and in order to do that a lot of individualism has to be worked out of every one of us. Any notion that people can have a primary responsibility for one person, that they can have that "out" — we have to destroy that notion in order to build a collective, we have to destroy all "outs" to destroy the notion that people can lean on one person and not be responsible to the entire collective. It's heavier than that, too, because it has to do with male chauvinism and male supremacy, and the development of woman's leadership, the development of women as communists. A lot of what's going on is people resisting the notion that in a collective everyone is equal. A lot of resistance comes from men, from men who have a privileged situation in that relationship, from men who dig the fact that they have control over another person. It comes from men who are involved in a classical pattern of male chauvinism, of finding a woman whom they can control, trying to teach that person, build that person up, take credit for building them up, begin feeling a lot of contempt for them, a lot of competition with them, and maintain that relationship to maintain their dominance. We have seen concretely that there is not an instance of a relationship that we've seen that doesn't have some kind of dominance in it, some kind of control over someone's acts — and for the most part, it's the woman who is held back. In practice, when people are operating in collectives and those relationships break down, the women begin to get strong, begin to assert themselves, begin to come out as leaders, not as political people who work through another individual, but as political people who build collectives and lead struggles. I think every one of us could run down instances like this. I'm from Michigan and could run down five or six instances, and I think that the women in Detroit are the strongest, most exemplary people in our movement right now, and I think it's precisely because they grappled with this issue early, they dealt with it four months ago, they got through it and understood the need to take the initiative in changing those relationships, and they did. That's an example, the most heated example of the job that we have to do. We have to organize ourselves in collectives, fight our individualism, we have to see that the Mellen-Hegel formula is true: freedom is the recognition of necessity, that we become free when we realize the tasks that we have to do and go about changing ourselves into the instruments that can do those tasks.

The other thing that's clear around the whole action is the question that Klonsky raised at the NIC when he said you guys aren't into serving the people, you're into fighting the people, and we kind of just sat there and said that that's wrong. We thought about the whole thing of serve the people, and we thought that you don't serve the people by opening a restaurant, or by fighting for a dollar more, you serve the people, that means all the people, the Vietnamese, everybody, by making a revolution, by bringing the war home, by opening up a front. But the more I thought about that thing "fight the people," it's not that it's a great mass slogan or anything, but there's something to it. What's true about it is that we've never been in a struggle where we didn't have to fight some of the people. For instance, at Michigan State we had to fight jocks, we had to fight a lot of them, and in the process of the next couple of weeks we won over a number of these jocks. We understood that they weren't our enemies, but we also understood that when they objectively acted like our enemies they had to be fought, and that that was the best way to deal with them. There's a lot in white Americans that we do have to fight, and beat out of them, and beat out of ourselves. And that part of it is true — we have to be willing to fight people, and fight things in ourselves, and fight things in all white Americans — white privilege, racism, male supremacy — in order to build a revolutionary movement. We know there's going to be polarization, but we also know that through that polarization there's going to be change. In Detroit, the whole question of creating a presence, of polarization, has come to a halt because they've polarized the whole city. They've been to every drive-in, every high school, and people have an opinion of SDS. How many places has anybody even heard of it? When you say SDS in Detroit, they say oh, those are those broads who beat up guys, or those are those people who come into drive-ins, and that polarization is an important thing. Of course, the pole of the city that hates us is all these old "movement people."

The major criticisms of the action have to do with adventurism, have to do with leading people to a slaughter, have to do with the pig rumor that we've been telling people that we're bringing guns to Chicago, and these things must be smashed, and it's a tricky thing to smash. It's a good rumor for them to pass around, because it does three things, highly contradictory. First they say we have guns, and that sets people up, so that they can attack us. It also scares people away, it makes people scared to get into it. But the third thing it does is that it forces us to take a defensive and a weak position on guns, it forces us to say no, we're not asking people to bring guns to Chicago. Do we dig guns? Well, no . . . It forces us into that defensive position. And when we make clear that we're not urging anybody to bring guns to Chicago, we're not urging anybody to shoot from a crowd, but we're also going to make it clear that when a pig gets iced that's a good thing, and that everyone who considers himself a revolutionary should be armed, should own a gun, should have a gun in his home.

Since our militance is going to obviously lead to a military confrontation, maybe not this year, then the fact that most of us in here don't even know karate makes us fools, and whoever doesn't own a gun and doesn't know how to use a gun is a fool. So we should state publicly that we believe in, we support, and we are preparing for armed self-defense, because that's what we have to do in order to win.

Our politics deals well with the question of adventurism, and we don't have to be defensive about the action. It's clear that the opposition to the action comes from right-wing "movement people." The unity of the opposition to the action is incredible, because people are uniting who have totally different positions. Anticommunists are uniting with people who call themselves Stalinists, are uniting with people who believe there's a black nation only in the South, are uniting with people who don't believe there's any black nation, and that whole unity is basically around one thing, and that's fear, basically around an inability to understand that we have to continue to move forward, and that we have to continue to build a fighting movement, and take that fight to the streets of Chicago, and take it back from Chicago to our local cities, and make them pay a price by involving thousands and thousands of kids in militant, out of sight destructive actions in every city in this country. So that this whole fall we begin to chip away at imperialism in the most concrete way that we can, and all the right-wingers who are united around this one thing, we should just ignore them — they're not our base, they never were, and they never could be. A strategy that talks about power is a strategy that ignores them and goes to the youth in the cities and begins to build among them.

I want to deal with one last criticism of the action, and that's what Klonsky puts forward in his famous article, "Why I Quit." What Klonsky says is that we didn't act on the mandate of the convention and build a united front action against the war. In the first place that's a lie, and a lot of the running dogs are going around saying we support the action except not really, the same way that PL says well, we dig struggle except where it really is. It's a lie to say that was passed at the convention because the paragraph that talked about the united front was debated at the convention and was dropped out of the resolution.

It's also important to understand that even if it passed, we wouldn't implement it because we understand that what we have to do is to build a movement that's geared toward power — and we're not going to be involved in obeying mandates that tell us to do something that's a losing strategy. For the first time in SDS a coherent leadership was elected, with stated politics, with coherent politics, stated before they were elected, and they're united on that. Not only are they united on that, but they're in a collective that has a base in probably the most important regions in the country, and that bigger collective, the Weather Bureau, makes political decisions, moves in a political way, and moves for victory, and it would be insane for anyone to expect leadership to organize around mandates and drop their own politics.

In the national office we're building a political collective for the first time. And it's a collective that understands that it has a primary responsibility to Weatherman, to the Weather Bureau, that its job is the implementation of those politics. And the people who don't believe that, or can't understand that, have been fired, or will be fired, because we're building a political movement, we're building a movement of revolutionaries, and we have to do that in a coherent way. The same is true of *New Left Notes*, which is looking better and better. The political content of the articles in *New Left Notes* has to speak to the best politics in the organization.

And I think that's important — that we have to organize around our politics, not around some mushy, directionless student movement, but around a movement of revolutionary youth, and we must begin to build revolutionaries in the movement, not just anyone who wants to join in the club, not just "movement people."

The criticisms of the action have to be dealt with in that honest way, in a very up-front way, have to be totally smashed, and people have to begin to get a sense that the politics of this action can win, are winning, can be built and are being built all over this country. In every city in the Midwest where we've got a summer program, people are predicting thousands and thousands of people coming out in October for the action, and that's thousands and thousands of people that we've never reached before — vets, greasers, bikers. At the Metro Beach action Motor City SDS got into a fight with a gang. But a week later the gang sent a message that they sure did dig beating up SDS but they also dig going to Chicago to beat up some pigs.

Strategically, in the long run, it's our overwhelming strength that we have to play off of and that we have to win people to, and we have to communicate to people, and that's the only way people are going to come to understand the reality of the fact that we can, and will, and beginning in October are going to bring the war home in Detroit, in San Francisco, in Columbus, and New York, and everywhere all over the country.

Appendix 2

In late May, 1970, the New York Times bureau in Chicago and Liberation News Service in New York received typewritten statements which claimed to be the transcript of a tape-recorded message from Bernardine Dohrn. The statement was the first released by the Weatherman leadership following the March 6 explosion, as well as the first since the Flint war council in December, 1969. The threat at the end of the statement was carried out on June 9, 1970, when a bomb caused heavy damage to the headquarters building of the New York City Police Department. The statement is dated May 21, 1970. The text is taken from the June 8, 1970, issue of the Great Speckled Bird.

HELLO. This is Bernardine Dohrn.

I'm going to read a declaration of a state of war.

This is the first communication from the Weatherman underground.

All over the world, people fighting Amerikan [the German "k" is a device used by radicals to suggest the United States is fascist] imperialism look to Amerika's youth to use our strategic position behind enemy lines to join forces in the destruction of the empire.

Black people have been fighting almost alone for years. We've known that our job is to lead white kids into armed revolution. We never intended to spend the next five or twenty-five years in jail. Ever since SDS became revolutionary, we've been trying to show how it is possible to overcome the frustration and impotence that comes from trying to reform the system. Kids know that the lines are drawn; revolution is touching all of our lives. Tens of thousands have learned that protest and marches won't do it. Revolutionary violence is the only way.

Now we are adapting the classic guerrilla strategy of the Vietcong and the urban guerrilla strategy of the Tupamaros to our own situation here in the most technically advanced country in the world.

Che taught us that "revolutionaries move like fish in the sea." The alienation and contempt that young people have for this country has created the ocean for this revolution.

The hundreds and thousands of young people who demonstrated in the sixties against the war and for civil rights grew to hundreds of thousands in the past few weeks actively fighting Nixon's invasion of Cambodia and the attempted genocide against black people. The insanity of Amerikan "justice" has added to its list of atrocities six blacks killed in Augusta, two in Jackson and four white Kent State students, making thousands more into revolutionaries.

The parents of "privileged" kids have been saying for years that the revolution was a game for us. But the war and racism of this society show that it is too fucked up. We will never live peaceably under this system.

This was totally true of those who died in the New York townhouse explosion. The third person who was killed there was Terry Robbins, who led the first rebellion at Kent State less than two years ago.

The twelve Weathermen who were indicted for leading last October's riots in Chicago have never left the country. Terry is dead, Linda [Evans] was captured by a pig informer, but the rest of us move freely in and out of every city and youth scene in the country. We're not in hiding, but we're invisible.

There are several hundred members of the Weatherman underground and some of us face more years in jail than the 50,000 deserters and draft dodgers now in Canada. Already many of them are coming back to join us in the underground or to return to the Man's army and tear it up from the inside along with those who never left.

We fight in many ways. Dope is one of our weapons. The laws against marijuana mean that millions of us are outlaws long before we actually split. Guns and grass are united in the youth underground.

Freaks are revolutionaries and revolutionaries are freaks. If you want to find us, this is where we are. In every tribe, commune, dormitory, farmhouse, barracks and townhouse where kids are making love, smoking dope and loading guns — fugitives from Amerikan justice are free to go.

For Diana Oughton, Ted Gold and Terry Robbins, and for all the revolutionaries who are still on the move here, there has been no question for a long time now — we will never go back.

Within the next fourteen days we will attack a symbol or institution of Amerikan injustice. This is the way we celebrate the example of Eldridge Cleaver and H. Rap Brown and all black revolutionaries who first inspired us by their fight behind enemy lines for the liberation of their people.

Never again will they fight alone.

May 21, 1970

Appendix 3

The following statement, titled "New Morning" after Bob Dylan's most recent record album, was sent to a number of underground newspapers in early December. It was signed by Bernardine Dohrn and accompanied by her thumbprint in order to establish its authenticity. The text printed here appeared in the December 17–January 6 (1970–71) issue of Rat.

December 6, 1970

THIS COMMUNICATION does not accompany a bombing or a specific action. We want to express ourselves to the mass movement not as military leaders, but as tribes at council. It has been nine months since the townhouse explosion. In that time, the future of our revolution has changed decisively. A growing illegal organization of young women and men can live and fight and love inside Babylon. The FBI can't catch us; we've pierced their bullet-proof shield. But the townhouse forever destroyed our belief that armed struggle is the only real revolutionary struggle.

It is time for the movement to go out into the air, to organize, to risk calling rallies and demonstrations, to convince that mass actions against the war and in support of rebellions do make a difference. Only acting openly, denouncing Nixon, Agnew and Mitchell, and sharing our numbers and wisdom together with young sisters and brothers will blow away the fear of the students at Kent State, the smack of the lower East Side and the national silence after the bombings of North Vietnam.

The deaths of three friends ended our military conception of what we are doing. It took us weeks of careful talking to rediscover our roots, to remember that we had been turned on to the possibilities of revolution by denying the schools, the jobs, the death relationships we were "educated" for. We went back to how we had begun living with groups of friends and found that this revolution could leave intact the enslavement of women if women did not fight to end and change it, together. And marijuana and LSD and little money and awakening to the black revolution, the people of the world. Unprogramming ourselves, relearning Amerikan history. The first demonstration we joined; the first time we tried to convince our friends. In the wake of the townhouse we found we didn't know much about each other's pasts — our talents, our interests, our differences.

We had all come together around the militancy of

young white people determined to reject racism and U.S. exploitation of the third world. Because we agreed that an underground must be built, we were able to disappear an entire organization within hours of the explosion. But it was clear that more had been wrong with our direction than technical inexperience (always install a safety switch so you can turn it off and on and a light to indicate if a short circuit exists).

Diana, Teddy and Terry had been in SDS for years. Diana and Teddy had been teachers and both spent weeks with the Vietnamese in Cuba. Terry had been a community organizer in Cleveland and at Kent; Diana had worked in Guatemala. They fought in the Days of Rage in Chicago. Everyone was angered by the murder of Fred Hampton. Because their collective began to define armed struggle as the only legitimate form of revolutionary action, they did not believe there was any revolutionary motion among white youth. It seemed like black and third world people were going up against Amerikan imperialism alone.

Two weeks before the townhouse explosion, four members of this group had firebombed Judge [John M.] Murtagh's house in New York as an action of support for the Panther 21, whose trial was just beginning. To many people this was a very good action. Within the group, however, the feeling developed that because this action had not done anything to hurt the pigs materially it wasn't very important. So within two weeks' time, this group had moved from firebombing to anti-personnel bombs. Many people in the collective did not want to be involved in the large scale, almost random bombing offensive that was planned. But they struggled day and night and eventually, everyone agreed to do their part.

At the end, they believed and acted as if only those who die are proven revolutionaries. Many people had been argued into doing something they did not believe in, many had not slept for days. Personal relationships were full of guilt and fear. The group had spent so much time willing themselves to act that they had not dealt with the basic technological considerations of safety. They had not considered the future: either what to do with the bombs if it had not been possible to reach their targets, or what to do in the following days.

This tendency to consider only bombings or picking up the gun as revolutionary, with the glorification of the heavier the better, we've called the military error. After the explosion, we called off all armed actions until such time as we felt the causes had been understood and acted upon. We found that the alternative direction already existed among us and had been developed within our collectives. We became aware that a group of outlaws who are isolated from the youth communities do not have a sense of what is going on, cannot develop strategies that grow to include large numbers of people, have become "us" and "them."

It was a question of revolutionary culture. Either you saw the youth culture that has been developing as bourgeois or decadent and therefore to be treated as the enemy of the revolution, or you saw it as the forces which produced us, a culture that we were a part of, a young and unformed society (nation).

In the past months we have had our minds blown by the possibilities that exist for all of us to develop the movement so that as revolutionaries we change and shape the cultural revolution. We are in a position to change it for the better. Men who are chauvinists can change and become revolutionaries who no longer embrace any part of the culture that stands in the way of the freedom of women. Hippies and students who fear black power should check out Rap Brown's *Die Nigger Die* and George Jackson's writings. We can continue to liberate and subvert attempts to rip off the culture. People become revolutionaries in the schools, in the army, in prisons, in communes and on the streets. Not in an underground cell.

Because we are fugitives, we could not go near the Movement. That proved to be a blessing because we've been everywhere else. We meet as many people as we can with our new identities; we've watched the TV news of our bombings with neighbors and friends who don't know that we're Weatherpeople. We are often afraid but we take our fear for granted now, not trying to act tough. What we once thought would have to be some zombie-type discipline has turned out to be a yoga of alertness, a heightened awareness of activities and vibrations around us — almost a new set of eyes and ears.

Even though we have not communicated about ourselves specifically before this, our actions have said much about where our heads are at. We have obviously not gone in for large scale material damage. Most of our actions have hurt the enemy on about the same military scale as a bee sting. But the political effect against the enemy has been devastating. The world knows that even the white youth of Babylon will resort to force to bring down imperialism.

The attacks on the Marin County Courthouse and the Long Island City Jail [October 10, 1970] were because we believe that the resistance and political leadership that is growing within the prisons demands immediate and mass support from young people. For all the George Jacksons, Afeni Shakurs and potential revolutionaries in these jails, the movement is the lifeline. They rebelled expecting massive support from outside.

Demonstrations in support of prison revolts are a major responsibility of the movement, but someone must call for them, put out the leaflets, convince people that it is a priority. We are so used to feeling powerless that we believe pig propaganda about the death of the movement, or some bad politics about rallies being obsolete and bullshit. A year ago, when Bobby Seale was ripped off in Chicago and the movement didn't respond, it made it easier for the pigs to murder Fred Hampton. Now two Puerto Ricans have been killed by the pigs in the New York jails, in retaliation for the prisoner rebellion. What we do or don't do makes a difference.

It will require courage and close families of people to do this organizing. Twos and threes is not a good form for anything — it won't put out a newspaper, organize a conference on the war, or do an armed action without getting caught. Our power is that together we are mobile, decentralized, flexible and we come into every home where there are children who catch the music of freedom and life.

The women and men in jails are POWs held by the

United States. When an Amerikan pilot is shot down while bombing North Vietnamese villages, he is often surrounded by thousands of people who have just seen their family and homes destroyed by the bombs he was delivering. Yet the man is not attacked and killed by the Vietnamese but is cared for as a prisoner. Nixon is now waging a last ditch moral crusade around the treatment of these Amerikan war criminals to justify all his impending atrocities.

The demonstrations and strikes following the rape of Indochina and the murders at Jackson and Kent last May showed real power and made a strong difference. New people were reached and involved and the government was put on the defensive. This month the bombings could have touched off actions expressing our fury at double-talking Laird and his crew — war research and school administrators and traveling politicians are within reach of our leaflets, our rallies, our rocks. Women's liberation groups can find in Nguyen Thi Binh a sister for whom there is love and support here. Her proposals for peace must be explained and Bloody Dick's plans to use more bombers to replace the GIs who are refusing to fight exposed as the escalation and genocide it is. Vietnamization Indianization limited duration protective reaction suppressive fire horseshit. It seems that we sometimes forget that in Vietnam strong liberated women and men live and fight. Not as abstract guerrilla fighters, slugging it out with U.S. imperialism in Southeast Asia, but as people with values and loves and parents and children and hopes for the future.

People like Thai, a fighter in the People's Liberation

Armed Forces who was in Hue during Tet and at Hamburger Hill a year later, or Than Tra, an organizer in the mass women's organization and the students' movement in the cities, who had not seen her lover in nine years. They traveled for a month to come to Cuba to meet with us, to sing and dance and explain how it is in Vietnam. There is nothing brutal or macho about guns and bombs in their hands. We can't help thinking that if more people knew about them, the anti-war movement would never have allowed Nixon and Agnew to travel to so many cities during the past election with only the freaks in Kansas State and the people of San José to make our anger at his racism known to the world.

The hearts of our people are in a good place. Over the past months, freaks and hippies and a lot of people in the movement have begun to dig in for a long winter. Kent and Augusta and Jackson brought to all of us a coming of age, a seriousness about how hard it will be to fight in Amerika and how long it will take us to win. We are all beginning to figure out what the Cubans meant when they told us about the need for new men and new women.

People have been experimenting with everything about their lives, fierce against the ways of the white man. They have learned how to survive together in the poisoned cities and how to live on the road and the land. They've moved to the country and found new ways to bring up free wild children. People have purified themselves with organic food, fought for sexual liberation, grown long hair. People have reached out to each other and learned that grass and organic consciousness-expanding drugs are weapons of the revolution. Not mandatory for everyone, not a gut-check, but a tool — a Yaqui way of knowledge. But while we sing of drugs the enemy knows how great a threat our youth culture is to their rule, and they employ their allies — the killer drugs (smack and speed) — to pacify and destroy young people. No revolution can succeed without the youth, and we face that possibility if we don't meet this threat.

People are forming new families. Collectives have sprung up from Seattle to Atlanta, Buffalo to Vermont, and they are units of people who trust each other both to live together and to organize and fight together. The revolution involves our whole lives; we aren't part-time soldiers or secret revolutionaries. It is our closeness and the integration of our personal lives with our revolutionary work that will make it hard for undercover pigs to infiltrate our collectives. It's one thing for pigs to go to a few meetings, even meetings of a secret cell. It's much harder for them to live in a family for long without being detected.

One of the most important things that has changed since people began working in collectives is the idea of what leadership is. People — and especially groups of sisters — don't want to follow academic idealogues or authoritarians. From Fidel's speeches and Ho's poems we've understood how leaders grow out of being deeply in touch with movements. From Crazy Horse and other great Indian chiefs we've learned that people who respect their tribe and its needs are followed freely and with love. The Lakotas laughed at the whites' appointing one man to be chief of all the Lakota tribes, as if people wouldn't still go with whichever leader they thought was doing the right thing!

Many of these changes have been pushed forward by women both in collectives with men and in all women's collectives. The enormous energy of sisters working together has not only transformed the movement internally, but when it moves out it is a movement that confuses and terrifies Amerika. When asked about the sincerity of Madame Binh's proposals Ky says, "Never trust a woman in politics." The pigs refuse to believe that women can write a statement or build a sophisticated explosive device or fight in the streets. But while we have seen the potential strength of thousands of women marching, it is now up to revolutionary women to take the lead to call militant demonstrations, to organize young women, to carry the Vietcong flag, to make it hard for Nixon and Ky to travel around the country ranting about POWs the same day that hundreds of women are being tortured in prisons in South Vietnam.

It's up to us to tell women in Amerika about Madame Binh in Paris; about Pham Thi Quyen, fighter in the Saigon underground and wife of Nguyen Van Troi; about Madame Nguyen Thi Dinh, leader of the first South Vietnamese People's Liberation Armed Forces unit uprising in Ben Tre in 1961; about Celia Sanchez and Heidi Santamaria who fought at Moncada and in the Havana underground; about Bernadette Devlin and Leila Khaled and Lolita Lebrun; and about Joan Bird and Afeni Shakur, and Mary Moylan here.

We can't wait to organize people until we get ourselves together any more than we can act without being together. They must go on at the same time. None of these changes that people are going through are rules and principles. We are in many different regions of the country and are building different kinds of leaders and organizations. It's not coming together into one organization, or paper structure of factions or coalitions. It's a New Nation that will grow out of the struggles of the next year.

Weather Underground